CANADA'S PARLIAMENT

A PRIMER

OTHER BOOKS IN THE COLLECTION

Political Law in Canada

The Senate of Canada

The Recognition of Two Official Languages in Canada

Federalism in Canada: Evolving Constitutional,
Political, and Social Realities

Drafting, Interpreting, and Applying Legislation

UNDERSTANDING CANADA

CANADA'S PARLIAMENT

A PRIMER

Steven Chaplin

IRWIN
LAW

INSTITUTE OF PARLIAMENTARY AND POLITICAL LAW
INSTITUT DE DROIT PARLEMENTAIRE ET POLITIQUE

Canada's Parliament: A Primer
© Irwin Law Inc, 2023

Published in 2023 by
Irwin Law Inc
Suite 206, 14 Duncan Street
Toronto, Ontario   M5H 3G8
irwinlaw.com

Cover image: Adobe Stock

ISBN: 978-1-55221-661-3 | e-book ISBN: 978-1-55221-662-0

Cataloguing in Publication available from Library and Archives Canada

Title: Canada's parliament : a primer / Steven Chaplin.
Names: Chaplin, Steven, author.
Description: Series statement: Understanding Canada | Includes bibliographical
    references and index.
Identifiers: Canadiana 20230208983 | ISBN 9781552216613 (softcover)
Subjects: LCSH: Canada. Parliament.
Classification: LCC JL136 .C53 2023 | DDC 328.71—dc23

Canadä

ONTARIO | ONTARIO
CREATES | CRÉATIF

Printed and bound in Canada.
1 2 3 4 5   27 26 25 24 23

For my wife, Ann; my children, Alastair and Leslie;

and for generations to come

Author's Note

On 8 September 2022, as this book was going to press, Queen Elizabeth II died, and King Charles III ascended to the throne. In present times, there are few direct consequences for Parliament, or for this book, other than reading all references to the Queen as the King, and the necessary references from Her to His.

But this was not always the case. Prior to 1867 for Canada, and 1843 in the United Provinces of Canada, on the demise of the sovereign, parliaments and legislatures were dissolved. One part of the Parliament, and the person who had summoned Parliament, ceased to exist, and therefore the Parliament came to an end. Similarly, various major players in the parliamentary process, including the Cabinet, would have to reswear oaths of office to the new sovereign in order to continue in their functions. These matters have now been settled by section 2 of the Parliament of Canada Act that provides "Parliament shall not determine or be dissolved by the demise of the Crown and, notwithstanding the demise, shall continue, and may meet, convene and sit, proceed and act, in the same manner as if that demise had not happened." Similar provisions in other federal and provincial statutes allow office holders to continue in their functions without interruption or the requirement to reswear any oath.

It is also worth noting that on the death of the Queen, the Houses of Parliament meet and offer their formal condolences to the King on the death of a person who was not only the Queen but also the parent of the new King. On 12 September 2022 King Charles III met with the two houses of the UK Parliament to receive their Addresses of Condolences and Loyalty. In His reply, the King recognized the centrality of Parliament in the UK constitution, and the responsibility of the King to maintain its role and functions:

> As I stand before you today, I cannot help but feel the weight of history which surrounds us and which reminds us of the vital parliamentary traditions to which members of both Houses dedicate yourselves, with such personal commitment for the betterment of us all.
>
> Parliament is the living and breathing instrument of our democracy. That your traditions are ancient we see in the construction of this great hall and the reminders of mediaeval predecessors of the office to which I have been called....
>
> While very young, Her late Majesty pledged herself to serve her country and her people and to maintain the precious principles of constitutional government which lie at the heart of our nation. This vow she kept with unsurpassed devotion.
>
> She set an example of selfless duty which, with God's help and your counsels, I am resolved faithfully to follow.

This reply, and the King's commitment, are reminders of the history and continuity that lies at the heart of the Westminster system of government as it has developed in both the United Kingdom and Canada — a peaceful and seamless change of head of state, and a major component of our democratic institutions. One that recognizes the past, confirms the present, and will allow for the necessary changes for the future.

September 2022

Contents

Contents

Foreword

In the Canadian system of Democracy, Parliament is the focal point of the state. It is the assembly that deliberates the country's great policy issues. It is also the institution that enacts the legislation that applies to the entire citizenry. Most importantly, Parliament is the sole body that can legitimately hold to account the government of the country. It perpetuates the link of legitimacy between citizen-voters and lawmakers. These are enormous responsibilities. As the Canadian Parliament, what the Senate and the House of Commons do to fulfill their respective roles is serious, methodical, and in many respects, continuous from one election to another. To those not actively participating, it may seem complicated, perhaps even distant from daily concerns, but quite to the contrary, Parliament is always relevant.

The question whether the public information about — and citizen knowledge of — Parliament rises to the level of its importance for all of society must be addressed. Regrettably, both information and knowledge are inadequate. The fact that public education is a domain of responsibility dispersed among the provinces and territories results in the teaching of widely diverse views about government. The fact that educational agendas must make time available for more current issues results in the overall decline of attention to governmental institutions and processes. Moreover, in an age when audio-visual methods of information have largely displaced the printed word, it is that part of parliamentary work that is most photogenic — namely, question period — that is best known. Citizens' impressions of the overall context and work of Parliament have consequently become distorted.

Despite current trends in public information and education, the relevance and importance of Parliament remain. This book is a vital response to the gap between demand for, and supply of, information and knowledge for all citizens. Steven Chaplin approaches the topic with over fifteen years' experience as a lawyer to the House of Commons, including as the House's litigator in several important court cases. He grounds his study in the historical origins of the Canadian Parliament, and he discusses each of the constitutional components of Parliament — the Commons, the Senate, and the monarch. As a discussion of Parliament would be incomplete without mention of political parties, that explanation is also included.

The core of this primer deals with the functions and purposes of Parliament. Almost all countries in the world have deliberative and legislative assemblies. The great interest of this examination of the Canadian Parliament lies in its analysis of how this particular deliberative and legislative assembly ensures that Canada is a Democracy. Over the century and a half of this country's history since Confederation, practices that were originally based on British precedent but are now specific to modern Canada have evolved. These ensure that from one election to the next, Parliament fulfills its functions and remains in a legitimate dialogue with the citizenry. These are matters that should be familiar to all participants in the national life of Canada. Everyone, including students, citizens, and those in the process of becoming Canadians, will benefit from a better understanding of how Parliament functions. This book provides that foundation.

Gregory Tardi
Editor, *Understanding Canada* collection
January 2022

Introduction

Canada is a constitutional Westminster democracy; as such, Parliament is at the centre of its constitutional system. Parliament is not merely a political body. Although often considered only as a legislature, it is more than that. In addition to legislating, it provides legitimacy to government, holds the government to account for its actions, approves all taxation and spending, and inquires into and debates all matters of public importance.

Although the roots of Canada's Parliament are firmly planted in British history, it has developed and evolved to meet the unique conditions of Canada. Parliament here must operate in a country originally conceptualized as one based on two languages, cultures, and legal systems, but that now strives to recognize the Indigenous peoples who lived on the land recognized as Canada, long before there was a Canada, with their own languages, cultures, and systems of government. Parliament must also function as part of a federal state, with provinces that have matured since Confederation in 1867.

As a modern state, Canada also strives to recognize the importance of individual rights and freedoms which, at times, are difficult to reconcile with the collective nature of parliamentary democracy.

It is also a fact that Canada is sometimes seen as living in the shadow of the United States. Much of the news, cultural influence, and political information in the public realm, particularly on social media, is American-centric. The expectations and experiences of many Canadians are based on views of the American system of government, albeit as seen through a Canadian lens. The result is a focus on strong individual political leaders who are a central pivot of government, with the centralization of power in the hands of the prime minister and a concurrent weakening of parliamentary institutions. Members of Parliament are seen and referred to as politicians, not parliamentarians, and party politics and parliamentary discourse are almost indistinguishable. Senators are considered nobodies at best, and cronies, patronage appointees, and political has-beens at worst.

At the same time, the press and public discourse often misuse terms, confusing the House of Commons with Parliament or government. The prime minister is often given the same status as a president. The Opposition is often ignored, or only referred to by its political party name, rather than as the Opposition.

The system is considered virtually dysfunctional. There are suggestions that the only way forward is to make radical changes to the institutions themselves, with abolition of the Senate and proportional representation as the leading candidates.

I am not so pessimistic, nor do I believe that radical change is necessary or optimal, not at least without a full understanding of how Parliament is designed and is supposed to function, and after expending the effort to make the existing institutions work as they were intended.

The place to start is to remind ourselves of what Parliament is, where it comes from, and how it functions. It is only then that we can ask ourselves how we move forward. Do we strengthen the existing system, expecting those who hold positions within them to do better and respect our form of government? Or do we need to make significant constitutional changes? In either case, we should make these choices with a better understanding of the form of government we currently have.

This short book is an attempt to at least set the baseline for that discussion.

CHAPTER ONE

History and Overview

Preamble

It is only fitting that we begin our study of the Parliament in Canada with the Preamble to the *Constitution Act, 1867*.[1] It states that Canada was formed "with a Constitution similar in Principle to that of the United Kingdom." These are not mere words. They have significance for the way Canada governs itself. The Preamble puts Parliament at the centre of the Constitution. To understand this, it is necessary to consider how and why Parliament is at the centre of the constitutional system of government in the United Kingdom.

English History — Early Development

A form of Parliament has existed in the United Kingdom for at least a thousand years. Although the term Parliament, as a description of a governing body, does not find its way into the English language until 1173, the genesis of an assembly-based system of governing pre-dates the Norman Conquest of 1066. By the time of *Magna Carta*, in 1215, which some believe to be the root of Parliament, both the basic form and purpose of Parliament had been set. The king governed with the advice of a council composed of barons and senior clerics. The making of law (in the form of decrees) the settling of major disputes, the determination of whether to wage war, and the means of support, either by money or provision of troops, was the business of the various assemblies held. What *Magna Carta* did was to formalize the state of the system to that point, and to have the king agree and sign it. An equally important, but less known companion document, the *Charter of the Forest*, was signed in 1217, during the regency of Henry III, when major barons acted on behalf of the underaged king.[2]

Both Charters were arrived at following a series of unresolved grievances between the barons and an unyielding King John. It was because long-standing grievances had not been resolved that the barons met King John at Runnymede in June 1215 to force the king, by signing *Magna Carta*, to acknowledge their grievances and to recognize the role that the barons had in deciding the affairs of the kingdom. This was closely followed by a period when it was necessary for the barons to act in the name of the young king. By the time Henry III came of age the role of the barons in governing had firmly rooted itself in the English Constitution. For example, twenty-five great councils of barons to conduct the business of state were held during the regency between 1216 and 1225.

One of the key terms of the initial *Magna Carta* was that there could be no taxation or supply of money without the approval of the barons, and further that the barons as a council must be summoned for this purpose. In 1225, the council insisted that King Henry III, now having reached majority age, agree to abide by all the terms of the two Charters, or the council would not agree to taxes. For the next fifty years or so, until these principles were fully accepted, the barons demanded the agreement of the king to abide by the terms of the Charters or they would not grant any money or agree to taxes. In 1275, the first *Statute of Westminster* was agreed to, which cemented the concept of "parliamentary" consent for taxation as a cornerstone of the English constitution.[3]

Initially, with few exceptions, only barons and the most senior bishops were summoned to the councils. However, in 1258, a summons for knights from each shire was issued. This was, in part, so that grievances of "commoners" could be brought and reported to Parliament. Also, such participation was likely to allow for greater acceptance of taxation and military participation. The prominence of participation by commoners was rapidly entrenched, and in 1283 the "commons" began to sit and discuss matters separately from the barons or Lords.

By the beginning of the fourteenth century, the basic framework for a Parliament composed of two Houses and the king was established. The actions and decisions of Parliament had to involve all three components of the structure. Consent for taxation from the two Houses, and particularly the House of Commons, was required. The presentation and addressing of grievances, petitions, and legal suits in return for supply (i.e., money) became the basis for the making of legal determinations, either in individual cases or as Acts of Parliament to address broader concerns of the realm and to put in place laws of general application. Since many petitions and grievances were based on various abuses of officials under the authority of the king, or on concerns that taxes had not been spent for the purpose they were granted, addressing these grievances also created a rudimentary form of accountability.

Although in theory Parliaments were supposed to be held on a regular basis, the reality was often one of a reluctant king summoning a Parliament only when he needed something, be it a change to a statute or, more likely, money. Kings were reluctant to summon a Parliament since the two Houses would make demands on the Crown to change laws and address various grievances relating to expenses or alleged abuses of power. In short, the king did not like to have his authority questioned, or his prerogative use of power curtailed. The struggle between the Houses of Parliament and the king was persistent and was exacerbated by the view taken by many monarchs that they had a divine right to rule. Their power came from God and it was therefore not proper for Parliament to try to restrict or constrain such powers.

By the seventeenth century the strain between Parliament, as the two Houses referred to themselves, and the king became untenable when Charles I refused to call a Parliament for eleven years. And when he was finally required to call one, he refused to accept numerous demands of Parliament that he saw as a challenge to his divine right to rule. The result of this confrontation was the English Civil War, Parliament convicting the king of treason and having him executed, and the establishment of the Commonwealth of England, without any monarch.

1689 — The Glorious Revolution and the *Bill of Rights*

The Commonwealth lasted from 1649 to 1660. This was followed by a short period of the Restoration of the monarchy. But it was not long before the kings began to try to reassert their authority. For various reasons, including the inability of James II to come to terms with Parliament, the king fled to France, effectively abdicating the throne. In the meantime, Parliament's preferred contender for the throne, William of Orange, had landed in the south of England. But before William could take the throne, Parliament insisted on his agreeing to terms that would make Parliament the supreme governing body and severely curtail royal authority. This would create a constitutional monarchy.

The result of the bargain was the *Bill of Rights, 1689*.[4] This Bill established, by Act of Parliament, who was to be king and the new line of succession. Parliament would from this point forward determine who would be the reigning monarch, ending any premise of the right to reign being divine. More importantly, the Act established an independent, supreme Parliament at the heart of English constitutionalism. The following provisions indicate the centrality of Parliament, and mark the decline of the Crown's ability to act without the authority of Parliament.

That the pretended Power of Suspending of Laws or the Execution of Laws by Regall Authority without Consent of Parlyament is illegall.

That the pretended Power of Dispensing with Laws or the Execution of Laws by Regall Authority, as it hath been assumed and exercised of late, is illegall;

...

That levying Money for or to the Use of the Crowne by pretence of Prerogative without Grant of Parlyament for longer time or in other manner then the same is or shall be granted is Illegall.

...

That Election of Members of Parlyament ought to be free
That the Freedome of Speech and Debates or Proceedings in Parlyament ought not to be impeached or questioned in any Court or Place out of Parlyament

...

And that for Redresse of all Grievances and for the amending strengthening and preserveing of the Lawes Parlyaments ought to be held frequently.

Laws were to be made by Parliament and the Crown could neither suspend nor dispense with any law. All taxation had to be approved by Parliament. There were to be free elections of members (albeit by a limited electorate) and Parliaments were to be held frequently. Most importantly, Parliament and its activities were to be free from interference from the courts and others, including the Crown and Crown officials.

These fundamental principles put Parliament at the centre of the English constitution. And by virtue of the Preamble of the *Constitution Act, 1867*, it is at the centre of the Canadian constitution as well.

Reforms to Democratic Institutions in England and Pre-Confederation Canada

Over time the English House of Commons became the centre of constitutional power. Means to control the business and outcome of Parliamentary debate, including the content of laws, and to limit and oversee the exercise of power by government were developed.

those attending readily agreed that the primary mode of governance would be rooted in an elected assembly, based on an equitable seat distribution by population, with a ministry primarily selected from among its members. That ministry would be accountable and responsible to the elected assembly. Similarly, many of the attributes of the Westminster system, such as taxation, legislation, and the relationship between the executive and the assembly, were taken as given to the extent that these relationships were not expressly referred to in the written text.

But the size disparity among the colonies needed to be addressed. It was this disparity, along with the relative power relationship between the provinces and the federal government, that presented the greatest challenges and were the major focus of the debate among the various attendees. The resolution came in both how the federal legislative institutions were designed and how powers and responsibilities were to be distributed between the federal government and the provinces. Both would have an impact on how Parliament and the legislatures would work. It would also be the reason that Prince Edward Island and Newfoundland did not initially join Confederation.

The structural solution included the creation of a bicameral (two House) Parliament, similar to that of the United Kingdom. The House of Commons would be popularly elected and be the House to which the government would be responsible. It was intended to act, look, and feel like the UK House of Commons. The number of seats in the House would be allocated by provincial population with a guarantee of seats to smaller provinces. In addition, there would be an upper house, the Senate, akin to the House of Lords, but with a Canadian twist. It would have senators appointed for life (now age 75), but there would be a limited number of senators, with the seats apportioned equally by region. Initially there were twenty-four senators each for Ontario, Quebec, and the Maritime provinces (Nova Scotia and New Brunswick). The Senate would have the ability to review, amend, or defeat any bill presented in either House. This would, in theory, provide regional balance and protect the smaller provinces from being overwhelmed by a system based solely on representation in a House founded on population. As the anticipated growth in population occurred elsewhere in Canada, the smaller provinces would always have their protected proportion of seats in the Senate.

The other sticking point was the allocation of legislative, and therefore government, responsibilities between the federal and provincial levels of government. The division of powers had to recognize the cultural and historic differences between the various colonies. In particular, the distinctive character of Quebec and the guarantees of language, education, religion, and legal system granted by the British one hundred years previously had to be respected. Quebec's concern for the probability that the French language and religion would shrink as Canada expanded also needed to be addressed. All provinces were leery of the potential for a centralizing of power by the federal government at the provinces' expense. The solution was to grant exclusive legislative authority over matters of local concern to the provinces while matters of national concern would be the business of the federal government. Matters of local concern encompassed education (including religion-based separate schools), management of local businesses, and the administration of property, family status, and legal systems. Since these legislative and government responsibilities were established as exclusive matters for the provinces, Parliament's legislative capacity and ability to govern in these areas was severely restricted.

Although Canada had a constitution similar in principle to that of the United Kingdom, the federal nature of the constitution, with two levels of government each having exclusive jurisdiction over different matters, and the requirement to treat provinces equitably, required a degree of deviation from the UK model. To allow for a federal state, the powers of Parliament were constitutionally limited by the powers allocated to provincial legislatures.

Canada's Parliament

Notwithstanding these federalism constraints, the component parts of the Canadian Parliament operate in a manner very similar to those of the UK Parliament. In addition to the Preamble of the *Constitution Act, 1867*, the Act provides for specifics on the structure and powers of Parliament.

The Parliament of Canada, according to the *Constitution Act, 1867*, consists of three parts: "the Queen, an Upper House styled the Senate, and the House of Commons." Since the Queen is not present in Canada, her functions and duties are carried out by her representative, the Governor General, who acts in her name. Like the United Kingdom, laws can only be made by Parliament — that is, all three entities acting together. This ensures that no one participant can make laws, including the government acting in the name of the Queen, without the authority of Parliament. All laws are enacted in the name of the Queen on the advice and consent of the Senate and House of Commons. This is formally known as the Queen in Parliament.

Each component part of Parliament has a role to play. The Canadian Parliament has the same structure as the UK Parliament, and the role played by each component is similar to that of their UK counterparts. When there is confusion or a gap in the written constitution, knowledge, practice, or precedent, it is not uncommon to look to the history and practice of the UK Parliament or to the relevant UK counterpart for guidance.

Each of the component parts will be looked at in more detail in later chapters; however, a brief sketch is provided here.

The Queen as Represented by the Governor General

The Governor General, as representing the Queen as head of state, has various roles to play in Parliament, some formal and ceremonial, some more substantive.

The Governor General is involved in the appointment of senators on the advice of the prime minister, summoning Parliament, calling on the person having the confidence of the House of Commons to form a government as prime minister, reading the Speech from the Throne, proroguing and dissolving Parliament, and issuing writs for elections. The Governor General is also involved, at least formally, in the legislative process, by granting Royal Recommendations for legislation requiring the expenditure of money, and the granting of royal assent. The granting of royal assent is the final legislative act in the passage of legislation. With the grant of royal assent, a bill becomes an Act. Royal assent is granted on the advice of the two Houses, unlike most acts of the Governor General, which are based on the advice of the Cabinet (as a committee of the Privy Council) or the prime minister. Although theoretically possible, no bill is even likely to not receive royal assent. The monarch has accepted the decision of the other two more representative bodies of Parliament since the early eighteenth century.

House of Commons

Although the Senate is constitutionally the upper house and therefore takes formal precedence over the House of Commons, Canada has evolved into a mature democracy, with the House of Commons, as the democratically elected House, now considered the central institution of Canada's parliamentary system.

The 338 members of the House of Commons, known as Members of Parliament (MPs), are simultaneously elected at a general election. If a seat becomes vacant between general elections, a by-election for that seat will be held to fill the vacancy. Members of Parliament are predominantly elected as representatives of a particular political party, with those members elected as representative of each party sitting together in the House of Commons as a caucus.

The composition of the House of Commons plays a critical role in determining who will govern. Following an election, one of the members of the House of Commons, usually the leader of the party holding the most seats in the House of Commons, is believed to be able to obtain the confidence or presumptive support of a majority of MPs. That person will be asked by the Governor General to form a government and becomes prime minister and leader of the government. The prime minister then selects the ministers who will be responsible for various parts of the government, including departments, and together they form the Cabinet.

So long as the government retains the confidence of the House of Commons, it has significant control over the agenda of the House. The vast majority of bills that are likely to become laws are introduced in the House of Commons by ministers of the government. Any bill that involves the expenditure of money also requires a Royal Recommendation, effectively Cabinet approval. Constitutionally, all bills that require the raising of revenue, taxation, or the expenditure of public funds must first be introduced in the House of Commons. As a result, much of the work of the House of Commons is focused on the consideration and passing of government bills, budgets, and estimates.

To manage its business, the House of Commons has several standing committees roughly based on broad portfolios, such as justice, government operations, and public accounts. As a bill passes through the House of Commons, it is studied in detail by a committee and possible amendments to the bill are considered and reported back to the House for final consideration. For many reasons, amendments are often not successful because the government commands a majority, or at least the confidence of the House. However, committees play an important role in studying the bills and bringing to the public's attention concerns with the bill that the government may need to pay attention to, at least, politically.

Once a bill has been voted on three times, the final version of the bill is sent to the Senate for the Senate's review, study, and vote.

Most people only see the House of Commons as a place where politicians pass legislation. But this is not the only function of the House of Commons. The government must retain the confidence of the House of Commons, and that confidence is constantly tested by way of open and public accountability. Ministers, including the prime minister, must be prepared to defend the government's actions and decisions in the House of Commons. This is referred to as the House's function of holding the government to account. The most obvious manifestation of this function is daily Question

Period when the members, other than ministers and parliamentary secretaries, have the opportunity to pose questions of the prime minister and ministers about the government's policies and decisions, and about the operations of the various ministries. Other ways that the House of Commons holds the government to account include committee inquiries on any matter within the committee's mandate, including specific actions or omissions in the operation of a government department. Committee reports can demand a government response.

Since the House of Commons is the body in which the prime minister and Cabinet sit and to which the government is accountable, it is the body that is the focus of public attention and is often wrongly referred to as Parliament. Since the members are elected, the general public is more engaged with members and the political happenings and consequences of the work of Members of Parliament and the House of Commons than with Senators and the Senate. At the same time, the work of the House can become very political and focused on political expediency.

As a counterbalance to the politically focused House of Commons, in Canada, there is a second House, the Senate, which plays a significant role as part of Parliament.

The Senate

The Senate is composed of 105 Senators. The allocation of seats is regionally based; twenty-four from each of Ontario, Quebec, the Maritime provinces combined (Nova Scotia ten, New Brunswick ten, Prince Edward Island four), and the Western provinces (Manitoba, British Columbia, Alberta, and Saskatchewan six each), six for Newfoundland and Labrador, and one each for the three territories. Senators are appointed by the Governor General on the advice of the prime minister. A senator is appointed once and sits until age 75 years.

The Senate's practices and procedures are similar to those of the House of Commons. A bill must receive three readings to pass the

Senate, and normally between the second and third reading, the bill is referred to one of the Senate's standing committees for detailed review and consideration. In some cases, the Senate, knowing that significant or time-sensitive legislation has been introduced in the House of Commons, will begin its committee hearings before the bill has passed in the House.

With the exceptions relating to the introduction of money bills (see Chapter 4), the Senate has the same legislative capacity as the House of Commons. Legislation can be introduced in the Senate and, if passed there, referred to the House of Commons for its approval. The Senate also reviews all legislation passed by the House of Commons. Through the Senate's three readings and committee hearings, Senators can propose amendments to bills that, if adopted by the Senate, will require that the bill be returned to the House of Commons for its reconsideration on the bill as amended. Only when both Houses agree on the text can a bill be recommended for royal assent. Failure to reach agreement will result in the bill not progressing to the royal assent stage. The Senate can also defeat a bill and thereby end the bill's progress through the legislative process. Although possible, such defeats or impasses are quite rare since the Senate recognizes that the House of Commons is the democratically elected chamber and is ultimately accountable to the people through elections. Sometimes threats of defeat or amendment slow down the process and focus the public's attention on the dispute with a view to getting the government to change its position, but in the end the Senate will normally yield.

This should not be taken to mean that the Senate serves no purpose, is impotent, or is a mere rubber stamp in the legislative process. The Senate is often referred to as the chamber of sober second thought. This is a relatively accurate description. Whereas the House of Commons is driven by politics and sometimes by political expediency, senators are not subject to the same constraints. Not being subject to the same political pressures, senators have the ability to carefully examine bills and provide less politically motivated suggestions for improvements.

Senators generally accept that it may not be their place in a democracy to block the policy initiative behind government legislation introduced in the House of Commons. However, they see their role as making the legislation based on that policy better. Through Senate review, bills, and therefore laws, can be improved.

Like the House of Commons, the Senate also has the power to inquire into, and make recommendations to the government on, any matter that falls within federal jurisdiction. It is this role at which the Senate has excelled. Since senators do not have to face elections and continue to hold their seats over a number of Parliaments, it is possible for the Senate to conduct in-depth studies over longer periods. With the benefit of time and little risk of political consequences, reports can be more comprehensive and contain recommendations that are not as politically motivated as may be the case when studies are conducted in the House of Commons.

Life Cycle of a Parliament

Parliament is not a continuous institution. A Parliament is called, or summoned together, following each general election, and is dissolved or ended in order to have the next general election. As a result, each Parliament is separate and distinct from other Parliaments. A Parliament lasts from the day it first meets until the date of its dissolution. At the time of writing, Canada is at the beginning of the 44th Parliament. Once it is dissolved, it will cease to exist, a general election will be called, and the 45th Parliament assembled.

A Parliament begins on a day determined by the Governor General, on the advice of a person the Governor General has asked to form a government as prime minister. All senators are invited to reconstitute themselves as the Senate in the Parliament, and all those who were elected in the general election are summoned to constitute the House of Commons for the Parliament. The Governor General will also attend the opening of Parliament, so that at the opening all three parts of Parliament assemble together. The Governor General reads the Speech from the Throne, which outlines the government's proposed agenda for the first session of the Parliament.

A Parliament can last for up to five years, but usually ends in dissolution before the expiration of five years. A Parliament is usually broken into sessions. At the time of writing, Canada is in the second session of the 44th Parliament. Each session ends with a prorogation. At the time that one session ends, the date for the next session is normally indicated. The Governor General, the Senate, and the House of Commons again meet together, with the Governor General reading a new Speech from the Throne for that session. Parliament cannot conduct any business during the period of prorogation. The date and length of a prorogation is determined by the prime minister, who advises the Governor General to prorogue Parliament to the next session date.

While Parliament is in session, the House and Senate each have sitting days that are set out in established calendars, although each House can amend its schedule of sitting days. Between sitting days each House is adjourned. When a House is adjourned, it is still in session and therefore can be recalled to conduct business without the need for another Speech from the Throne.

Constitutionally, a Parliament must sit at least once a year.

Parliament ends with a dissolution. The date of the dissolution is determined by the prime minister advising the Governor General to dissolve Parliament. The advice to dissolve Parliament is given at the discretion of the prime minister. However, if the government loses the confidence of the House of Commons, the prime minister will almost always ask that Parliament be dissolved. By convention, the Governor General will accept the prime minister's advice, unless it is soon after the election and the government loses a vote of confidence shortly after the Parliament's initial Speech from the Throne. In such circumstances the Governor General might ask another member, usually the Leader of the Opposition, to try to form a government, rather than having an election so soon after the previous one.

Once Parliament is dissolved, it ceases to exist. There is no Parliament, therefore no parliamentary functions can take place. The

Senate is suspended, and all Members of Parliament cease to be members. Following a dissolution, a general election is called to elect the individuals who will be Members of Parliament in the next Parliament. At the dissolution of Parliament, a writ for the election of a Member of Parliament is issued for each constituency. Those who seek re-election do not do so as Members of Parliament. They are, like all seeking to be elected, simply candidates. Once the ballots are counted in a constituency, the writ is endorsed with the name of the person who received the most votes. These individuals will be summoned to form the next House of Commons.

Sovereignty and Supremacy

It is not uncommon to hear the terms "parliamentary sovereignty" and "parliamentary supremacy" used when discussing the relative place of Parliament within the Canadian constitutional architecture. It is also not uncommon for the terms to be used incorrectly as interchangeable. Although somewhat related notions, they are not the same, particularly in Canada where there is a written constitution that empowers different levels of government with exclusive authorities and grants specific rights that can act as a constraint on legislative capacity.

Sovereignty is about capacity. Supremacy is about relative power. Sovereignty allows a body the capacity to act within its authority without any other body or person being able to interfere with or override the actions or decisions taken. Historically, the UK Parliament was said to enjoy parliamentary sovereignty in that it could make any law about any matter. Neither the courts nor the government could ignore the law or overturn it. Whatever the Commons, the Lords, and the monarch decided together was the law. No other body, other than Parliament, could change it. Parliament had full, inexhaustible capacity to make law. There may have been moral or political checks, but there were no legal ones.

In Canada, sovereignty is divided between the federal and provincial levels of government. Sections 91 and 92 of the *Constitution*

Act, 1867, in particular, set out the relative powers in such a way as there are no gaps in legislative capacity. All power, and therefore all sovereignty, is divided between the two levels of government. What one level of government cannot do the other can. At the same time, the exercise of each type of power is exclusive to the level of government to which it is assigned. Although there may seem to be much overlap, constitutionally, what one level of government can do, the other cannot. To this extent, the sovereignty of each level of government is limited by the legislative capacity of the other.

In 1982, the sovereignty of each level of government was further limited by constitutional amendments, including the *Canadian Charter of Rights and Freedoms*,[6] which entrenched certain rights within the Constitution. Parliament could no longer legislate in violation of such rights, and any law that violated the rights was of no force and effect to the extent of the violation.

So, there are two types of constitutional constraints on parliamentary sovereignty in Canada: federalism and the rights and freedoms entrenched by the *Constitution Act, 1982*, which included the *Canadian Charter of Rights and Freedoms*. Otherwise, if Parliament is exercising a power granted it and the law does not violate a constitutional right, its sovereignty is intact. Neither courts nor the government can strike down or alter a law because of the policy, effectiveness, or other difficulties they may have with it.

Supremacy, as distinct from sovereignty, is about who gets the last word on settling the law. Again, historically this was the king, then the king in Parliament. Parliament was the highest legal authority and therefore enjoyed parliamentary supremacy. It was considered the High Court of Parliament. In the end, Parliament could resolve any legal dispute, generally by statute or on a case-by-case basis. While the capacity to determine individual cases has passed to the courts, in the United Kingdom the last vestige of this power was the fact that until 2009, the House of Lords could hear cases and appeals. This power was abolished with the creation of the Supreme Court of the United Kingdom.

In Canada, the same degree of supremacy has never quite existed since there have always been constitutional constraints on the exercise of powers by Parliament. It has always been the role of the courts to determine whether Parliament had exceeded its jurisdiction by legislating in areas of provincial jurisdiction. Since the adoption of the *Charter of Rights and Freedoms* in 1982, courts have the power to determine if Parliament has exceeded its powers by legislating in such a way as to violate constitutional rights and freedoms. As a result, it has been said that in Canada parliamentary supremacy has been replaced by constitutional supremacy.

There are still, however, circumstances when Parliament is supreme. So long as it legislates within its constitutional authority, Parliament can enact legislation that creates or changes the law, including reversing court decisions on the law or modifying the consequences of court decisions for future cases. In an emergency, or in certain specified and temporary circumstances, this allows Parliament to act, even if to do so would ordinarily or otherwise be prohibited by the Constitution.

Parliament's Relationship to Other Constitutional Actors

Parliament is the central pillar in the Canadian constitutional architecture. In a democracy, it is proper that the institution with the largest elected component should be. It also means that all other constitutional actors have a relationship with Parliament.

Parliament's relationship with the government is the closest. The ministers, who collectively form the government, emerge from the elected House of Commons. The government is accountable to the House of Commons. Every minister is answerable to the House of Commons for their department and various government agencies, tribunals, and commissions assigned to their charge. Each minister is also accountable, as members of the Cabinet, for the decisions of the Cabinet. Collectively, they must constantly have the confidence of the House of Commons, and if confidence is lost, the government must resign and an election for a new House of Commons be called.

Ministers, as the government, are also responsible for the carrying out of the functions and duties prescribed by legislation. They are responsible for the management of government departments and agencies created and empowered by Parliament to conduct various tasks and make decisions required by legislation. They are also responsible for making the various regulations authorized by Parliament and for exercising administrative powers given to them by statute. And it is to Parliament that they must account for the carrying out of all of these functions.

The government also introduces the bulk of legislation within the House of Commons. It has control over the agenda of the House but must work with members of both Houses to ensure as smooth a passage of legislation as the processes and the necessary parliamentary scrutiny will allow.

The relationship of Parliament to the courts is more indirect. The simple outline of responsibilities within the Constitution is that Parliament makes the law, through legislation, and courts interpret the law and ultimately determine its application. Since Confederation, courts have been able to determine whether legislation falls within the matters assigned to Parliament's jurisdiction. Since 1982, courts have had a broader basis on which to consider the constitutional validity of laws where it is alleged that a law violates a right or freedom. These rights and freedoms are stated in relatively broad terms with a scope that people can disagree about, but which the courts ultimately determine. At the same time, the rights are not absolute, and Parliament has a margin of discretion if it can be shown that the limits on the rights in legislation are demonstrably justified. With the entrenchment of constitutional rights and freedoms, this relationship has become more complicated and has sometimes taken on a feel of confrontation tempered by dialogue. In this way the role of the democratic institution of Parliament is reconciled with the rule of law and the protection of rights, which is the domain of the courts.

The courts also play a role in protecting the independence of Parliament through ensuring that the constitutional privileges of Parliament and its members are respected and protected. Parliament has the constitutional ability to carry out its business without interference from the courts or anyone else outside of Parliament. As such, the courts cannot interfere, or allow anyone else to interfere, in the business of Parliament. In short, no one is able to use the courts or their processes to restrict members from attending or participating in proceedings or to censor them for anything done in proceedings. Nor can anyone attempt to use the courts to slow down or meddle in the passage of legislation, or in committee proceedings. The courts will ensure that Parliament is free to conduct its business.

Parliament's Accountability to the Electorate

Constitutionally, Parliament appears to be, and is, powerful. There are few legal constraints on its activities. Courts may, for limited purposes, be able to invalidate or limit the effects of legislation. But they cannot do so on political or policy grounds. One can imagine laws being passed, or decisions taken, that damage society but do not necessarily violate constitutional rights or boundaries. In contemplating such scenarios, one is left to consider whether there are means to limit Parliament from acting in such a manner. Succinctly put, the answer is democracy and elections. The greatest constraint on parliamentary and government action is political. Governments and parliamentarians are ultimately accountable to the people through elections. There are many ways that a policy can be achieved through legislation. The form and limits of the legislation implementing the policy are tempered and shaped by public opinion and potential electoral consequences.

This public accountability takes on numerous guises in parliamentary activities, including political party formation, leadership contests, electoral success, caucus formation, government formation, and legislative agenda setting. The political and electoral activities carry through into the business of a responsible Parliament. For all the activities of Parliament, consideration of the electorate is in the background. In a democracy, it is healthy for the electorate to continue to play a role, or at least to be considered, when the government puts its agenda to Parliament and Parliament holds that government to account. This is as important between elections as it is at the time of a general election. Elections are measured in weeks, Parliaments in years.

CHAPTER TWO

The Functions and Purposes
of Parliament

The Central Role of Parliament

Parliament is the focal point for the entire democratic, political, governmental, and legal structure of Canada. It provides the democratic legitimacy to government. It grants authority to the government to act and has the responsibility to hold the government to account for the exercise of that authority. It is the only body that can levy taxes and authorize the spending of public funds. It has exclusive authority to make laws. If courts provide interpretations on the application of laws not acceptable to Parliament, Parliament can recalibrate the laws to its liking. It is the only body that has the power to remove judges from the bench. It carries out these functions in a representative capacity for the citizens of Canada, and it is ultimately accountable to the electorate for its actions and decisions.

Parliament is composed of the Queen, as represented by the Governor General, the Senate, and the House of Commons. It is only when all three work together that Parliament can be said to act. No single component, nor two acting together, has the capacity to claim to act as Parliament. When Parliament meets together, the Queen represents the state and all of its authority, the Senate represents provincial and regional interests, and the House of Commons represents individual Canadians. As Canada has matured as a democracy the relationship between these three components has changed. The Governor General, as representative of the Queen, plays less of a direct role; however, they retain particular roles in the formation of government and remain a constant reminder of the importance of constitutional continuity regardless of the political configuration of the government of the day. The Senate, with senators appointed until age 75, is no longer seen as representative of the provinces, as provinces have evolved and developed their own direct relationship with the federal government. The Senate, however, continues to provide continuity within the Houses of Parliament, providing stability and consideration of legislation from a more detached perspective. The House of Commons, composed of members who are directly elected, has continued to evolve as the pre-eminent House as democratic principles and rights have gained prominence. As a result, that House is the body that is most connected to the government of the day, responsible for considering and acting on the policy mandate of the electorate, and in turn is accountable to the electorate for the decisions taken by Parliament. This heightened role has led to a greater centralization of power in the prime minister and Cabinet, because they enjoy the confidence of the House.

Legitimacy

Parliament gives legitimacy to both laws and those charged with administering them. The House of Commons is composed of members elected by universal suffrage. This provides democratic legitimacy and consent for the enactment of legislation, the imposition of taxes, and approval of spending. Implicit in the election of a Member of Parliament is that those who elect them will abide by the laws enacted, and pay taxes as lawfully imposed. Members collectively are also responsible for determining who will be prime minister, and for continually holding the prime minister and the government to account for administering legislation, taxation, spending, and programs approved by Parliament. This responsibility provides the legitimacy for the various ministers to carry out the functions assigned to them by legislation, and to act on behalf of all Canadians. At the same time, those with whom the government interacts know that the authority of the government is backed up by the support and confidence of the House of Commons, the elected manifestation of the Canadian public.

Members of Parliament are directly accountable to those who elect them. As a result, they are effectively a conduit between Parliament and the public. They bring concerns of their constituents to the government and Parliament. They also communicate the work of Parliament to their constituents. Even though these communications are often flavoured by partisanship, the communication still takes place. When legislation or taxation is proposed, members will communicate the proposals to their constituents. Through this communication constituents voice their concerns, show their support, and make suggestions. Members can then express these concerns in parliamentary discourse. The sum of these interactions across the country provides members with the capacity to understand and act on a broad basis of national interest. Once a bill becomes legislation, members are also engaged in communicating the result to constituents, and explaining how the various interests were addressed within the legislative process. This continuous dialogue also adds legitimacy to, and implicit buy-in for, the outcomes of the parliamentary process.

The Senate also plays a role in providing legitimacy, particularly regarding legislation. As a body that reviews bills received as passed in the House of Commons, the Senate provides a second set of eyes and considerations in the legislating process. It can affirm, modify, and improve proposed legislation. Senators do not need to fear losing their seats in an election. As a result, the Senate also acts as a check on the political excesses of the House of Commons, or government, which may have acted in haste or as a result of political pressures, and thereby overlooked potential harm to those affected by the proposed law. Senators generally enjoy a greater luxury of time to study bills and seek to have the government and the

House revisit areas of concern. Despite senators not being elected, the work of the Senate, particularly when pushing back on a bill received from the House, draws the attention of the press and the public. This attention can put political pressure on the House to reconsider. This work plays a critical role in ensuring that the best legislative outcomes are achieved. It provides Canadians with further confidence in the legitimacy of the resulting law.

The Functions of Parliament

The functions of Parliament fall broadly into two categories: legislating and accountability.

Legislating

CONSTITUTIONAL LIMITS

There are two aspects to legislating: formal constitutional capacity and the exercise of legislative powers within that capacity.

Only Parliament and legislatures have the constitutional capacity to make laws. This has been the case since the *Bill of Rights, 1689*[1] and has been continued in Canada through the Preamble of the *Constitution Act, 1867*,[2] which provides that Canada enjoys a constitution similar in principle to that of the United Kingdom. The *Constitution Act, 1867* also sets out that Parliament has the exclusive authority to make laws for Canada, and the provincial legislatures have similar exclusive authority to make laws for the provinces. Although there is a common law tradition in all provinces except Quebec that results in resolving cases based on judicial reasoning and determined legal principles, any aspects of law that have been settled by the courts under that system are subject to being modified or annulled by legislation. In this way the constitutional supremacy of Parliament and its exclusive capacity to make laws manifests itself.

Because Canada is a federal state, legislative authority is divided between the federal Parliament and provincial legislatures. The different levels of legislative authority are set out in the *Constitution Act,*

1867 in such a way as to divide legislative capacity between Parliament and the legislatures. Each level of government is provided with exclusive powers to legislate in the areas assigned. The division of powers is such that there are no gaps, and that the full scope of legislative power within Canada is assigned to one level of government or the other. While there may seem to be overlap between the two sets of powers, this is not the case. Laws may complement each other. Different aspects of an activity may be governed by laws enacted by both levels of government. But such laws cannot conflict. When applying laws, the courts will strive to find a way for laws from both levels of government to work together harmoniously and to allow for the broadest scope of legislative authority for each level of government. However, when the conflict is not resolvable, the courts will determine which level of government has the legislative capacity to regulate the activity. It is not the purpose of this book to set out how the courts make these determinations. It is, however, important to understand that the Constitution places a subject matter-based limit on the legislative capacity of both Parliament and legislatures. The challenge is to understand and determine where the boundary lies.

When the *Constitution Act, 1982*[3] was enacted, it included the *Canadian Charter of Rights and Freedoms* (*Charter*).[4] The *Charter* sets out various rights and freedoms commonly found in the bills of rights of most western democracies and in international human rights treaties and declarations. The *Charter* includes democratic rights to vote and be elected and places limits on the length of a Parliament. It entrenches freedoms such as the freedom of expression, assembly, and association. It creates criminal law protections from unreasonable searches, affirms the presumption of innocence and fair trial rights, as well as the right to fair administration of laws and the right not to be deprived of life, liberty, and security of the person without fair process. It also sets out equality rights. Other parts of the *Constitution Act, 1982* provide for Indigenous rights, both historic and based in treaties.

The *Constitution Act, 1982* and the general principles of constitutional interpretation ensure that any legislation that infringes these freedoms and rights is of no force and effect to the extent of any infringement. As such, the protection of these freedoms and rights can be seen as further limits on legislative capacity.

At the same time, section 1 of the *Charter* and related jurisprudence provide the opportunity for legislation to have an impact on rights and freedoms where the limits can be justified in a free and democratic society. Again, the nuances of the tests for justification for such limitations and their application is beyond the scope of this book. But, given the importance that such rights have taken on since they were included in the Constitution, the consideration of potential infringement of rights and possible justification for that infringement have had a significant impact on the business of legislating.

THE NATURE OF LEGISLATING

The consideration of proposed legislation occupies most of the time of Parliament. Legislating, the presentation and enactment of bills, is the process Parliament follows to make laws. The result is an Act of Parliament, meaning that both Houses of Parliament have adopted the same language of a bill and the Governor General has given royal assent to the bill becoming law. Unless an Act says otherwise, the law as enacted comes into effect at the time it receives royal assent.

Legislation is the way that a government implements policy and regulates activity, either directly by operation of the law itself, or by means of enforcement through legal processes. Legislating is purposive. The purpose is either to change existing laws or to create new normative obligations and frameworks. Legislation is generally responsive to a problem or issue that has come to the attention of Members of Parliament, particularly those in government. A proposed solution, in the form of a bill, is a particular response to the problem based on a deliberate choice from among various possible options. A bill is a formal proposal for legislation presented to Parliament. Most bills are introduced in the House of Commons.

Legislation usually sets out its purpose and principles, establishes norms and conditions to meet the purpose, and provides for some form of administration and enforcement of the norms with regard to those affected by the Act.

One type of legislation involves the authority to tax and spend. Such legislation forms part of the implementation of the government's budget and includes taxation and fees, expenditure on equipment and the running of government, and the provision of benefits such as employment insurance and grants. A second type of legislation focuses on the activities of individuals, businesses, and other entities, and includes various forms of regulation or prohibition. Regulatory legislation would include the establishment of safety, production, and employment standards, environmental requirements, and licensing based on certain criteria. This type of legislation is often managed and enforced through administrative processes, including boards, commissions, or agencies to make decisions on the establishment of standards, the issuing of licences and permits, and the hearing of complaints. Such bodies often provide direction and can impose penalties to ensure compliance. Other Acts and legislative provisions set out norms to be followed or prohibit certain activities, with the failure to adhere to the norms or prohibitions resulting in an offence leading to fines or imprisonment. Criminal law, drug offences, and serious or intentional breaches of regulated activities fall within this type of legislation.

Only Parliament can make laws. However, legislative time is scarce and the need to return to Parliament every time any change is required, regardless of how minor, would be cumbersome. Therefore legislation will often authorize the government to make and amend regulations and make decisions to further the purposes of the Act. Regulations made pursuant to legislation are referred to as delegated or subordinate legislation. Regulations and decisions must comply with the legislation. The making of decisions or regulations must fall within the scope of the Act's provisions granting the power to do so. Regulations cannot amend or be made contrary to the substantive provisions of the Act.

While Parliament retains the ability to oversee that regulations are consistent with Parliament's intent, the number of regulations makes oversight more difficult. In providing government the author-ity to make delegated legislation, Parliament often has to balance accountability with efficiency. There are, however, some checks built into the making of regulations that help restrain government over-reach. For most regulations, there are requirements that the gov-ernment consult with those affected, and Parliament retains the capacity of oversight, often through complaints by those whose activities are regulated, to ensure that regulations remain consistent with the intention of Parliament as expressed in the Act.

Legislation is intended to apply to the entire country and all those who engage in the activity that falls within the purpose of the law. Since people are engaged in numerous activities, and activ-ities are often complex and interrelated with the activities of others, legislation involves the consideration and balancing of many factors, rights, and interests. As both a policy-based and legislating activity, the search for the right balance can best be summed up as establish-ing the best legal framework for the common or public good. While there is likely to be considerable debate over what the common good is, or what is in the public interest in any particular circumstance, the theory is that all participants in the legislating process believe that they are acting in the public interest for the common good.

Focusing on the common good requires an understanding that, as a parliamentarian engaged in legislating, one is not acting to further one's own interests or merely to further the interests of one's constituents. The common good requires an examination and con-sideration of the best interests of all those affected by the legis-lation, which is a national constituency, or a definable subset of the national body politic. In short, parliamentarians legislate for the entire country, with a view to what is best for the country as a whole, even if the result is one that may not prioritize, or that may even compromise, the interests of their own constituents.

Since parliamentarians are elected or appointed from different regions with different constituencies, the various interests of all Canadians can be weighed and considered in ascertaining the com-mon good. By having representation from across the country, the effects of proposed legislation on particular groups or constituents will be brought to the attention of the House and considered during the legislating process. However, in the end, determining the common good requires consideration of how the needs of others, not just one's constituents, are to be met.

The consideration of proposed legislation, first by the policy centres of government that prepare legislative proposals, then through instructions to drafters of bills, and finally by Parliament, involves the balancing of rights and interests of all who may be affected by the legislation. Considerations include the purpose for legislating, the objectives of the proposed legislation, how it will be implemented, and the effects of the legislation. At the same time that particular legislation is being studied, it is being examined for its compatibility with the existing law and the effects it may have on that law and the legal system as a whole. This includes the various rights, freedoms, and responsibilities found in the constitution, legislation, and international treaties and norms.

While rights instruments are often seen as a burden or limit on legislative capacity, legislation should also be seen as the means to achieve outcomes that promote, advance, or sustain constitutional rights and freedoms. In a liberal democracy, rights, freedoms, and responsibilities are the fundamental expression of the common good. They are the foundation for what it means to be a citizen within such societies. As such, they are more aspirational than restrictive. Legislation that focuses on the common good will allow for each individual in society to fully participate and achieve their potential to exercise their rights and freedoms and place responsibilities on the more privileged to protect the rights of others and seek reconciliation with those whose rights have historically been ignored or trampled.

Legislating is no small task and is a greater responsibility than mere representation of one's own self-interest, the interests of a particular group, or that of a small geographic constituency. Such goals can only be achieved by cooperative, albeit partisan, work and careful reflection in both Houses of Parliament. Legislation also requires thoughtful preparation by government ministers supported by a professional and neutral public service.

Although most legislation is prepared for presentation to Parliament by government ministers after considerable work and study by the public service, this does not mean that the legislative outcome of a bill should be considered as determined in advance. There is a significant role to be played by Parliament as it studies, dissects, and proposes amendments to bills. The following chapters on the House of Commons and the Senate explore how each House carries out their functions when legislating. As will be shown, their role is neither procedural nor a mere step toward the government always getting what it wants.

While this book only focuses on the role and function of Parliament, there are many steps within the public service and the government before bills are introduced. These processes often become the focus of parliamentary inquiry as a bill passes through Parliament. In a 2018 decision of the Supreme Court, one justice set out the "ideal" legislative process for legislation. Not all steps will necessarily be followed to their fullest, nor will they necessarily proceed in the order that they are listed. Each piece of legislation has its own purpose, complexity, and timeline that dictates the order in which and the degree to which each step is adhered to.

Department (Preparation)

1. The department prepares analyses and plans; ministerial approval is required to proceed with policy consultations.

Prime Minister, Cabinet and Department

2. The Prime Minister reviews and approves machinery-related issues (where applicable).
3. The sponsoring Minister makes a decision on the policy options and recommendations to Cabinet.
4. The memorandum to Cabinet is prepared.
5. The memorandum to Cabinet is subject to interdepartmental consultation.

6. The memorandum to Cabinet is approved by the Deputy Minister and senior management.

7. The memorandum to Cabinet is approved by the sponsoring Minister, and sent to the Privy Council Office.

8. The Privy Council Office briefs the chair of the Cabinet Committee.

9. The Cabinet Committee considers the memorandum to Cabinet, and the Privy Council Office issues a Committee Report.

10. Cabinet ratifies the Committee Report, and the Privy Council Office issues a Record of Decision.

11. The Department of Justice prepares a draft bill with the assistance of the legislation section drafting team, the sponsoring department, and the departmental legal services unit.

12. The bill is approved by appropriate senior officials in the sponsoring department.

13. The sponsoring Minister reviews and signs off on the bill.

14. The Government House Leader reviews the bill.

15. The Government House Leader seeks delegated authority from Cabinet to approve the bill for introduction.

16. The Privy Council Office issues the bill.

The House of Commons

17. The Government House Leader gives notice of the bill's introduction.

18. The bill is introduced in the House of Commons: first reading.

19. The bill proceeds to second reading (approval in principle).

20. The bill is considered in Committee (clause by clause consideration).

21. The Committee reports on the bill, including any recommended amendments.

22. The bill proceeds to third reading and final approval by the House of Commons.

The Senate

23. The bill is introduced in the Senate: first reading.

24. The bill proceeds to second reading (approval in principle).

25. The bill is considered in Committee (clause by clause consideration).
26. The Committee reports on the bill, including any recommended amendments.
27. The bill proceeds to Third Reading and final approval by ... the Senate.

Royal Assent

28. The bill receives royal assent from the Governor General.
29. The legislation (now a statute) comes into effect upon royal assent or (if the statute so provides) at a later date.

Operation of the Legislation (Department and Cabinet)

30. Regulations are made and decisions are taken pursuant to the authority conferred by the legislation.[5]

In addition to these steps there are also certain procedural and legal steps related to the Constitution that need to be followed. For all bills introduced by the government, the minister of justice is required to prepare and file a statement outlining the constitutional implications, if any, of the bill. This statement is to be presented to the House in which the bill is first introduced. In addition, if a bill requires the expenditure of any public funds or the imposition of taxes, the bill must be first introduced in the House of Commons, and where there is an expenditure of funds, the bill must be accompanied by a Royal Recommendation. A Royal Recommendation is essentially Cabinet approval. These two particular procedures will be discussed in the chapter on the House of Commons.

Throughout the process of legislating, the public servants who were involved in the policy discussions and promoting the bill within the government will often be called as witnesses before the committees in each House to explain the bill to members and senators. They will also brief ministers and parliamentary secretaries for their speeches to the House and Senate, and for their appearances before committees. Where amendments are proposed for bills, the public service will consider them and advise the minster on their effect so that the minister can determine the government's support or response.

Meanwhile, the various caucuses, members, and senators will have their advisers assisting them in preparing their responses and potential proposed amendments.

Accountability

One of the hallmarks of the Canadian parliamentary system of government is that the government (prime minister and ministers) is accountable to the elected House of Commons. While there are certain types of accountability associated with the legislative process in the Senate, the most consequential forms of accountability remain with the House of Commons. Accountability is inextricably tied to the concepts of confidence and responsible government.

Responsible government was the result of pressure from political reformers in the eighteenth and nineteenth centuries. And with any form of responsibility comes accountability. Two major forms of responsibility form interrelated parts of parliamentary government in Canada. From a constitutional governance perspective, responsible government includes the premise that the person called on by the Crown (in Canada, by the Governor General) to be prime minister is the person who enjoys the confidence of the House of Commons. The prime minister is solely responsible for the appointment of cabinet ministers to form the government. If the prime minister and the government lose the confidence of the House, they will resign and normally Parliament will be dissolved and an election held. Since the government has the confidence of the House, it is responsible and accountable to it. At the same time, the House of Commons is composed of elected members, each of whom will be held accountable as a candidate in the next election for both the government's and their own actions in the previous Parliament. First the government is accountable to the House of Commons, then ultimately to the public. With expansion of the franchise (i.e., those who can vote) to all citizens and with the expanding use of social media, a member's need to balance both responsibilities to the House and to the public becomes trickier.

This book focuses on the responsibility and accountability that the government has to the House of Commons. However, it would be naïve to not take into account the fact that all of the parliamentary actors in the House, as elected representatives, always keep one eye on the public's potential political response. This is true for both the government and the Opposition. The perceived reaction of the public undoubtedly influences the government's policy and legislative agenda, as well as the degree and focus of the Opposition's criticism and proposals for amendment. As one considers the various roles and procedures that follow, it is always wise to bear in mind that political considerations are often at play and will mitigate legislative and parliamentary responses.

PARLIAMENTARY AS OPPOSED TO PUBLIC ACCOUNTABILITY

The Westminster system of government is a parliamentary, not a public or popular, democracy. This means that decisions about who governs are made by Parliament, not the public. Each member of the public, through elections, chooses a member of the House of Commons. The public does not elect who will lead the government, either as an individual or as a party. It is the makeup of the House of Commons, composed of each of the 338 (2021 number) individually elected members that determines who will govern. As a result, the government, as composed of the prime minister and other ministers, is accountable to the House of Commons, not the electorate. Even in a subsequent election, each former member is only directly held accountable in their constituency. The degree to which electoral accountability is based on the past performance of the government, the proposed political agenda of each party for the future Parliament, or the individual appeal or performance of a particular candidate is a question that political scientists are better able to determine. And it may vary from election to election and from constituency to constituency. In any event, it will be for the newly elected House of Commons composed of the next

338 members, in the next Parliament, to determine who will govern and for how long.

In a formal, legal, and constitutional sense the government is only accountable to the House of Commons, and that accountability is a dominant feature of the work of any Parliament.

To form a government, a prime minister must enjoy the confidence of the House of Commons. Confidence is demonstrated by majority support of members of the House of Commons. Although the person who has the confidence of the House usually is the leader of the party caucus (i.e., group of members elected from the same party) with the most seats in the Commons, it is possible for a person who leads a smaller caucus to form a government, if they enjoy the combined support of other smaller caucuses sufficient to make up a majority. The person who enjoys the confidence of the House becomes the prime minister and forms a government by choosing ministers, who by convention now almost exclusively hold seats in the House of Commons. Although ministers can be senators, except for a government representative in the Senate to help shepherd bills through that chamber, ministers are rarely appointed from among senators.

With the prime minister and ministers sitting in, and forming part of, the House of Commons, they are available to be held accountable on a regular and continuous basis. This is different from most republican systems of government, like that of the United States, where the executive, comprising the president and cabinet, is separate and distinct from the legislative branch. The integration of the executive ministers within the House of Commons is what makes the body a Parliament, a place of discussion and accountability in addition to legislating. With the ministry forming part of the House of Commons, there is a greater connection between the elected House of Commons and the functioning of the government. Ministers are not only available and required to answer questions and defend the decisions and actions of the government, they also play an active role in the presentation and defence of proposed legislation, budgets, taxation, and spending.

Parliament, and in particular the House of Commons, has developed various means and procedures to hold the government to account, for both the way it governs and its legislative and financial agenda.

Because of the continuous accountability of the government, there is a symbiotic relationship between the government and the Opposition within Parliament. To reflect this, the House has structured itself to allow for a formal Opposition that is recognized, organized, and resourced. As a result, the Opposition, in many ways, is as important to the functioning of constitutional democratic government in Canada as is the executive government. The person who leads the largest caucus that is not part of the government is recognized as the Leader of the Opposition. As such, that person receives additional salary, support, and resources to carry out their functions. They also are given leading roles in the business of the House. They lead off questions in Question Period. After the prime minister, they are given primary speaking positions on major debates without the usual time limits. They are consulted on certain important appointments and may be briefed on serious matters in times of crisis.

The Leader of the Opposition also designates members of their caucus as Opposition critics for each of the ministers. Each critic is responsible for tracking the actions, decisions, and departments of their minister counterpart. After the leader, the critics often lead the questioning of ministers in the House, organize responses to bills, and follow the work of relevant committees. On the political front, the party caucus of the Leader of the Opposition is seen as a "government in waiting" and the party likely to form the government in the event that the party of the government is defeated at the next election.

Although the best known manifestation of accountability is the daily Question Period, there are more parliamentary ways in which the government is held to account for its operations as well as its proposed legislative agenda. These include members formally posing written questions that must be answered in writing. Usually these questions require a longer, more detailed, and often statistic-laden response. The answers may lead to follow-up oral questions, or provide information that allows a focused and considered response to a bill or in committee.

While the government generally controls the agenda for the House of Commons, there are certain designated days, referred to as Opposition or supply days, on which the Opposition determines the matter to be discussed. The Opposition can also bring motions of confidence. If the government loses such a motion, it must resign, and an election will likely be called. Finally, during debate there is often time for questions following speeches during which members can pose questions "for clarification."

Committees are also a major forum for in-depth consideration and questioning of government operations and legislation. Some consider committees the place where the real work of Parliament takes place. Committee work, while still somewhat partisan, is generally more collegial with a greater attempt at consensus reports. There are some committees in the House of Commons that are specifically focused on "holding the government to account," such as the Standing Committee on Public Accounts and the Standing Committee on Government Operations. Not only are they focused on accountability, they are chaired by a member of the Opposition.

Committees are free to establish their own timetables, subject to any time limits imposed by the House or Senate directly or by the Standing Orders and Rules. They often call witnesses from government departments, private sector experts, interested organizations, and individuals. These witnesses can provide a wide range of perspectives, from official government positions to evidence of how those who might not have been consulted by the government will be affected by a government policy, decision, or proposed legislation. Witnesses often provide suggested amendments for members to propose. Committees are provided with the broad power to send for persons, papers, and records. Most often, documents are within the control of the government and are provided by government witnesses. Once produced, the committee may base further inquiry on them. Sometimes the documents and witnesses may be from outside the government. Since witnesses are often interested in contributing to policy debate, they readily comply with committee requests. However, if the documents are not provided or witnesses do not appear the committee may request that the House or Senate issue a summons for the documents or witnesses. A summons from the House or Senate has the same effect as a court summons, and continued refusal is a contempt of Parliament and may be punished.

Once a committee has completed its inquiry, it can issue a report to the House or Senate with proposals for government action or with amendments to bills. It is not uncommon for a report to seek a response from the government with a fixed timeline. If a report is agreed to by the House or Senate, failure of the government to respond can result in various orders and resolutions, including, in the case of the House of Commons, a vote of non-confidence leading to the government's defeat.

The broad mandate of committees, combined with the power to obtain documents, results in a powerful forum for holding the government to account.

Officers of Parliament

There are also certain officers of Parliament that have been established to assist in holding the government to account. Most officers of Parliament are responsible for investigating and reviewing government activities, such as spending (Auditor General), protection and access to information (Privacy Commissioner and Information Commissioner), and protection of official languages (Commissioner of Official Languages). In addition, the Chief Electoral Officer is an officer of Parliament whose mandate is to ensure that there is no government involvement in elections. Unlike departments and other administrative agencies that report through ministers to Parliament, officers of Parliament report directly to Parliament. This means that they are significantly more independent of government ministers, and they can be relied on by Parliament to provide it with unbiased information. The timing of reports to Parliament are at the discretion of the officer and are referred directly to the appropriate committees.

Usually, the appointment and dismissal of officers of Parliament require at least consultation with the leaders of the various caucuses, and some require parliamentary approval. It is also possible, in some cases, for a committee to request that an officer investigate particular activities and report back to the House. Although there are often calls and proposals to add to the list of officers of Parliament on that basis that the proposed agency or body should be more independent of government, so far there has been reluctance to do so. This is because the degree of independence is only one aspect of the function of officers. It is even more significant that the role be seen as assisting Parliament with oversight of government operations.

There are other officers that assist Parliament in its functions, such as the Conflicts of Interest and Ethics Commissioner, the Senate Ethics Officer, and the Parliamentary Budget Officer. These officers function within Parliament and focus on the role of members, senators, and the business of each House. The Ethics Commissioner has a role in assisting the House of Commons in administering the ethics code for members. A similar role for the Senate is played by the Senate Ethics Officer. The Parliamentary Budget Officer has a role that is akin to that of the Auditor General. Whereas the Auditor General is responsible for reviewing how the government spent, or misspent, resources in carrying out its operations, the parliamentary budget officer is responsible for providing information to Parliament on the cost of proposed government spending (the budget) and the cost or revenue associated with any proposed legislation. In short, their job is to ensure that Parliament has an independent assessment of the financial consequences of any legislation it is asked to pass. In 2017, the ability to review the costs and revenue projections of election promises was added to the functions of the Parliamentary Budget Officer.

Most of the activities of the House, the Senate, and committees are public. The reports of officers of Parliament are made public once tabled in Parliament, although specific investigations are not conducted in public. In exceptional circumstances, particularly those involving national security or sensitive personal information, committees may conduct business behind closed doors, and report in such a way as to maintain protection of the particular information. Since committees are composed of members representing all caucuses in the House or Senate, any attempts to abuse this power are likely not to succeed. The review work of committees and officers of Parliament also provides the press and the public with the ability to judge the activities of both the government and the Opposition. Ultimately, the electorate will decide whether members should be held accountable through the ballot box.

Constitutional Amendments

Parliament is a major participant in the process of amending the Constitution. There are various formulae for amending the Constitution, depending on the complexity and impact on the constitutional architecture and the number of provinces affected by any amendment. Except for the amendment of a provincial constitution, which only requires the approval of that province's legislature, all of the formulae require the adoption of a resolution to amend the Constitution in one or more provincial legislative assemblies and the involvement of Parliament. The process for such amendments can begin with a resolution in a provincial legislative assembly, the Senate, or the House of Commons.

Although the amending process anticipates a resolution being adopted in both the Senate and the House of Commons, it is possible for the Constitution to be amended without approval of the Senate. If the necessary resolution is adopted in the House of Commons but is not adopted by the Senate within 180 days of the House resolution (excluding any period of prorogation or dissolution), the House can repass the resolution with the effect of allowing the amendment to proceed.

Once the necessary resolutions of the required provincial legislative assemblies and Parliament have been adopted in identical terms, the Governor General is informed, and will issue the necessary proclamation of the amendment.

Independence of Parliament

Parliament is composed of three entities: the Queen, the Senate, and the House of Commons. All three components are independent of each other, and it is only when they act together that they act as Parliament. Each of the component parts is independent of the Crown (as the executive or government) and the courts. As a result, they are free to act as the House, the Senate, and together as a Parliament without interference from either the government or the courts. Neither the government, as government, nor the courts can tell the House, Senate, or Parliament what it can consider, how to carry out its business, or hold to account any member, senator, committee, or participant in parliamentary business for anything said or done in Parliament. This generally also extends to the administration that supports each House. This allows each House and Parliament to carry out their work without fear of retribution or obstruction.

Parliamentary Privilege

The protection of the independence of Parliament from the Crown and the courts is primarily through what is referred to as parliamentary privilege. Privilege allows members, senators, and witnesses to be free to attend and participate in the business of Parliament, and to do so without fear of legal or administrative consequences.

Parliamentary privilege has been defined as "the sum of the privileges, immunities and power enjoyed by the Senate, the House of Commons and provincial legislative assemblies, and by each member individually, without which they could not discharge their functions."[6] As early as 1818, these privileges were extended by the House of Commons in the UK to include witnesses and others who participate in or are necessary for parliamentary proceedings. Parliament and its participants must be able to carry out their functions without obstruction, molestation, or interference. Although some privileges are seen as being applicable to members or participants, all privileges are in fact privileges of the Senate or House of Commons, and therefore only those bodies can waive them.

One misconception is that the privileges and rights provide an exception or exclusion from the law. This is not the case. They form part of the general and constitutional law of Canada. They have the same force and effect as any other aspects of the constitution, including the division of powers and the rights and freedoms found in the *Canadian Charter of Rights and Freedoms.* Privileges are not for the specific personal benefit of any individual, such that the individual is placed above the law. Privileges are necessary to allow Parliament to carry out its constitutional business freely. It is true that the actions, proceedings, and speech in proceedings cannot be reviewed in the courts. As a result, each House is responsible for making sure that its members do not abuse the protection. Since the privileges belong to the House, a failure to control members is a failure of responsibility by the entire House.

Parliamentary privileges have existed from earliest times and started to come into focus in the fifteenth century, when it was becoming more common for kings to charge, imprison, and sometimes execute members who spoke against the king in Parliament. Grievances and bills that challenged the authority of the king, or the refusal to do the king's will in Parliament, also attracted retribution by the Crown. Privileges developed to insulate members from such reprisals by the king and his courts. Privileges were first confirmed in a statute in 1512[7] and were included in Article 9 of the *Bill of Rights, 1689.* That Article provides that freedom of speech in Parliament is protected and that proceedings in Parliament cannot be impeached in any court or place out of Parliament, including in administrative proceedings.

Privileges have also been asserted by the House or Senate and respected by the courts to stop other forms of interference with Parliament, such as attempts to intimidate witnesses, attempts to stop testimony, or punishing witnesses for having testified. Other privileges preclude a member or participants in proceedings from being summoned by the courts while Parliament is in session, thereby taking them away from their participation in Parliament.

Although privileges protect proceedings in Parliament from being questioned elsewhere, this does not mean that the final decisions of Parliament, in the form of Acts, cannot be considered by the courts or applied in a manner that might not have been contemplated by Parliament. Enacted laws may also be judicially reviewed and potentially found to be constitutionally or legally inoperative. Government officials and bodies must interpret laws in carrying out legislated mandates. Courts can judicially review government decisions made pursuant to a statute to ensure government compliance with the law. Courts can also consider whether Parliament exceeded its constitutional powers. Such reviews and interpretations, however, can only take place after legislation is enacted. Judicial review cannot be used to interfere with or second guess the legislative process, including the reasons for taking certain steps, the effects that the steps may have on the legislative outcome, or the content of what is said by any individual participating in a parliamentary proceeding. For example, the courts have refused all attempts to compel consultation during proceedings, or to stop bills from being passed, or prevent royal assent from being given as the final step of the legislation process. In all cases, courts have indicated that they would be prepared to look at the content of the legislation for compliance with the constitution or applicable laws, but only after enactment.

Parliament's Relationship to the Courts

The relationship of Parliament to the courts has two main components: recognition and protection of privilege, and interpretation and application of legislation.

PARLIAMENTARY PRIVILEGE IN THE COURTS

As noted in the previous section, parliamentary privilege protects speech and proceedings from being questioned or impeached in the courts. These are constitutional protections, and therefore the courts will apply them to the same extent that they protect, interpret, and apply other aspects of the constitution as the supreme law in Canada. Since privileges are constitutional in nature, the courts should consider them whether or not they are specifically raised in a court proceeding. This principle is included as a section in the *Parliament of Canada Act*.[8] At the same time, privileges have limits. In a proceeding where privileges are at issue, courts must first determine the existence and scope of the privilege. To do so they will determine whether the privilege existed in the UK House of Commons at the time of Confederation, or whether the privilege is necessary to protect the business of Parliament from interference. An example might be the court determining the meaning and scope of what is a "parliamentary proceeding," and the degree to which the activity claimed to be protected by privilege is related to a proceeding. Once a matter is determined to be covered by privilege the inquiry of the courts ends. Courts cannot examine how the privilege was exercised within Parliament, or what took place within the "proceeding" or Parliament.

Based on the application of privilege, the courts have not allowed lawsuits for defamation or other claims based on what was said or done in a proceeding. They have not been prepared to review parliamentary proceedings, for example, to determine whether a committee treated a witness fairly. They will not stop any process in the development or consideration of proposed legislation, nor will they stop royal assent from being given. They will quash a non-criminal court summons, a witness summons, or a jury summons issued to members and senior House staff necessary to support proceedings when the House is in session. Usually, where the attendance of a member, as a witness, is important to a court proceeding, an agreement between the House and the parties to the case is made to allow the summons to have effect when the Parliament is adjourned. Courts will also protect witnesses by quashing any penalty or discipline that might be imposed against a witness by their employer based on the witness's appearance before a committee.

One difficult area of legal consideration is the application of statutes to either proceedings in Parliament or to the administration that supports the Senate, the House, or Parliament. As concerns proceedings, or matters covered by privilege, unless legislation specifically indicates that it applies to Parliament, it does not. Courts therefore cannot make any order that would result in the application of legislation to matters covered by privilege. This means that how a statute might apply within a proceeding is up to the Senate or House of Commons to decide. Most parliamentarians are aware of the principles behind various statutes, such as privacy, human rights, and national security, and will strive to protect those interests within the parliamentary context and within proceedings. However, if it is decided by the House or the Senate or their committees to not apply the principles within a proceeding, or to apply the principles differently from how a court might in non-parliamentary contexts, there is no recourse to the courts to review such decisions.

SUB JUDICE CONVENTION

While courts refrain from interfering in the business of Parliament, there are procedures and conventions that curtail parliamentary involvement in the administration, procedures, and decision making of the courts. It is up to the courts, not Parliament, to determine legal cases. Both the House and the Senate have put in place certain rules to ensure the courts are not interfered with. The first is the *sub judice* convention. This convention precludes Members of Parliament or Senators from raising or discussing matters that are before the courts for determination. Failure to adhere to the convention could result in the inability to empanel an impartial jury, place undue public pressure on the courts, or diminish the public's respect for the courts. It is also likely to confuse the public with respect to the respective roles of Parliament and the courts. Parliament is responsible for making the laws, and the courts for interpreting and applying them. Similarly, judges will not respond to a summons to appear before a parliamentary committee to discuss any particular decision, or how they might make determinations in the future. A second aspect of the convention is that members or senators cannot contact or otherwise take steps to influence a judge, court, or administrative decision maker on any particular case. Any such interference could be seen as both a contempt of court and a contempt of Parliament, which would subject the member or senator to discipline.

USE OF PARLIAMENTARY MATERIALS IN COURT PROCEEDINGS

Until the mid-1970s there was a general rule that courts would not look at the debates of the House of Commons or Senate when interpreting legislation. It was the settled view that since Parliament spoke with a collective voice, the way that it spoke was through legislation or specifically worded resolutions. How could courts determine which speeches of the 400-plus participants to consider? Members spoke for themselves, not Parliament. When interpreting or applying statutes, the courts were responsible for searching for Parliament's intention, not any individual member's intention.

Then, two things changed. The first involved courts looking for a way to determine the meaning of a statutory provision when faced with language that was truly ambiguous, where legislation could be read two equally plausible ways. The second was the adoption of the *Charter* that protected rights and freedoms but allowed Parliament to place legislated limits on those rights and freedoms so long as the limits were reasonable and demonstrably justified. Both these circumstances resulted in the greater use of debates (*Hansard*) and other parliamentary material in court proceedings. However, in each case the use is restricted to the purpose for which the material is allowed, all the while bearing in mind that the material is not to be used to question or impeach the proceedings.

In the case of searching for parliamentary intent, the use of parliamentary material must be to resolve a real ambiguity in the meaning of some textual language, and only when most other means of interpreting a statute have been exhausted. When faced with such a position, the court will only look to those speeches or debates that the court believes are reliable and will show intent. This usually involves an examination of speeches or testimony by the person who introduced the bill or amendment at issue, often the minister who is responsible for it. Other material that might be considered is the testimony of departmental officials who are called at committee to explain the legislation to committee members. If the provision being considered is an amendment, the court might look at the speeches of the member or senator who introduced the amendment in order for the court to ascertain the purpose or intent of the amendment in the context of the bill. Since the purpose of the court is to determine Parliament's intent, this exercise is not considered questioning or impeaching the proceeding; rather it is a means to arrive at a conclusion consistent with the proceeding.

The use of parliamentary material in assessing the reasonableness of legislated limits on *Charter* rights and freedoms is also an exercise to determine Parliament's "thinking." When assessing whether a limit is reasonable the courts will generally seek to determine how the provision is linked to the overall statutory scheme, including the options considered, and whether the option chosen was that which minimally impaired the right.

Has the government in its proposed legislation, and Parliament in its consideration of the legislation, justified any limits on constitutional rights and freedoms? To make these determinations a court may be required to examine how a matter proceeded through Parliament, the scope of the witnesses called, and the tenor of the debate and explanations for why the proponents of legislation chose the options that they did. There is now also a requirement that the minister of justice table a statement in the House in which any government-sponsored bill is introduced, outlining the minister of justice's position on the constitutional impact of the proposed legislation. This statement and Parliament's use and response to it may become a focal point for a court's consideration of how Parliament dealt with these issues.

This can be seen as a constitutional dialogue between Parliament and the courts on the permissible limits on rights and freedoms. If the court is not satisfied, it is possible for the court to find that rights have been infringed, but suspend its declaration for a period of time to allow Parliament to re-enact the suspect legislation in a manner that respects rights. When a court suspends a declaration it usually outlines how the legislation violated the right or freedom and why the limit fell short of justification. The court also recognizes that there are various ways for legislation to achieve a particular goal, and that how to do so is a choice for Parliament. Parliament can choose to revise the legislation to meet the court's concerns. The subsequent parliamentary proceedings often focus on meeting the court's concerns. And the dialogue continues, with the court, if there is a follow-up challenge, examining how Parliament addressed the concerns and whether the revised legislation is now justified.

Although less common when legislation does not affect rights and freedoms, the courts may also examine parliamentary materials in other constitutional contexts. Sometimes the line between federal and provincial jurisdiction is not clear, and legislation adopted at each level of government covers various aspects of an activity. It may be necessary for courts to determine if Parliament was aware of whether a bill, if enacted, would violate provincial jurisdiction, and whether there was a proposed way to read the federal legislation so as to dovetail or respect provincial jurisdiction while carrying out a federal purpose.

Parliament's Relationship to the Government

Parliament's relationship to the government is multi-faceted. It is one of both independence and coordination.

A common misconception is to confuse Parliament or the House of Commons with the government. The House of Commons is not the government. One of Parliament's fundamental roles is to hold the government to account. To do this it must be independent of the government and free to criticize and challenge the government. The House and the Senate also enjoy administrative independence so that the government and its departments, agencies, and other administrative bodies cannot control or influence them by application of government policies, information gathering, and budgeting.

ADMINISTRATIVE INDEPENDENCE

There are statutes that relate to the administration and management of the government. This legislation empowers various ministers to make decisions on how the government is to operate, how the government is to spend money for its own needs, and how its workforce is to be managed. Such legislation allows ministers to control the government's operations, spending, and administrative priorities. If this legislation were to apply to Parliament, ministers could make decisions that would interfere with the constitutional functions of Parliament.

The application of statutes to the administration that supports Parliament and parliamentary institutions is more complex. Many statutes are administered by government departments and agencies. If such statutes were to apply to Parliament, government decisions made pursuant to such statutes could result in restrictions on the operations of parliamentary institutions, restrict funding and therefore the operations of Parliament, allow for inspections that interfere with the business of Parliament, or could require the provision of information held by Parliament to the government. Since the administration of the House and the Senate works for the Opposition as well as members who support the government, care must be taken in applying statutes to avoid providing the government with the capacity to restrict the Opposition, or to provide access to information that might be used to restrict opposition. Application of statutes that would have such an effect could be seen as an interference with the independence of Parliament. If a parliamentary institution has any such concerns, they are likely to not adhere to the jurisdiction of the government agency, on constitutional grounds, and force the government to work with the administration to develop unique processes to apply the principles of the statute, while maintaining the independence and privileges of Parliament. In many cases, statutes are made or amended to include specific provisions dealing with the administration of parliamentary institutions. Specific areas covered by these statutes include employment rights for parliamentary employees and a regime that allows for parliamentary institutions to manage their financial, administrative, and security affairs separately from the government.

The House, Senate, and other parliamentary institutions therefore are responsible for their own administration, budgeting, spending, and human resources. They are also responsible for ensuring that members, senators, and caucuses are adequately resourced to carry out their functions. As independent constitutional actors, each member or senator needs the resources to do their job, which includes holding the government to account. Again, this resourcing cannot be determined by the government, and it therefore falls to each House to provide resources and rules to limit spending to the fulfillment of the member's parliamentary functions. To establish, manage, and oversee the administration of the House of Commons and the Senate, as well as members and senators, each House has established a body composed of members from all caucuses to make these decisions. For the House of Commons this is the Board of Internal Economy and for the Senate, the Standing Senate Committee on Internal Economy, Budgets and Administration. Although the government will have members on each of these bodies, their role is not similar to that of ministers. They act as a member of the body to ensure that each House and its members has the ability to carry out their functions.

In addition, since the House of Commons, the Senate, and Parliament are not the government, legislation that applies to a government department, or to the Crown generally, does not apply to them. Legislation must specifically include parliamentary entities. And even then, the inclusion must be carefully tailored to ensure the independence of Parliament is protected. To avoid confusion, separate legislation, or parts of legislation, are enacted to apply in the parliamentary context.

HOUSE AND SENATE BUSINESS

As noted above, one of the constitutional functions of the House of Commons, and to a lesser extent the Senate, is to hold the government to account through questions, debates, proposed amendments, and committee work. This opposition role is fundamental to the functioning of Parliament and the Westminster system of government.

At the same time, the government has the confidence of the House of Commons and has the legitimacy to govern. This includes a mandate to advance its legislative agenda within Parliament. It enjoys various priorities and benefits both by convention and pursuant to the Standing Orders of the House of Commons. The government sets the agenda for Parliament through the Speech from the Throne. Flowing from this agenda-setting, most legislation proposed is government bills. These bills occupy the majority of the time of the House of Commons, the Senate, and the various committees. The government presents the budget and sets the financial course for the country. It also sets out the estimates for spending. All legislation that involves spending requires approval of ministers through a procedure known as a Royal Recommendation, which is obtained through the Cabinet processes. While it is true that the various bills, budgets, and estimates must be approved by Parliament, so long as the government enjoys the confidence of the House of Commons, the government will ultimately obtain its objectives.

In addition to controlling the agenda of the House of Commons, the government often has the ability to control the work and agendas of most committees. Committee membership is based on the percentage of seats that each party's caucus holds in the House of Commons or Senate. Normally, at least in the case of the House of Commons, the government caucus has the most seats and therefore the most seats on committees. When there is a majority government, the government enjoys the support of a majority of seats on committees. The majority of members on a committee controls the agenda of the committee. This means that legislation passes more smoothly through committees and that there is less pointed study and criticism of government activities.

The public pays most attention to the bills before Parliament that might affect them directly, for example, criminal law and personal taxation. However, the majority of legislation involves the structuring of government programs and the regulation of business, trade, the economy, the environment, and health care. Legislation frames the nature and programming of government departments, agencies, boards, and commissions. It grants authority to public officials to make decisions, administer programs, and make regulations. Legislation also sets out which minister is responsible for the administration and implementation of the legislation.

REGULATION MAKING AND OVERSIGHT

A particular aspect of legislating intimately connects Parliament to the government. Legislation often sets out broad objectives and principles but leaves the details to regulation. Regulations are often referred to as delegated legislation and have the same force of law as does the legislation that authorizes them. Such legislation, in effect, gives the authority to the government to make law without that "delegated legislation" being subject to parliamentary approval before it is made. Consequently, governments often seek broad powers to make regulations. Although Parliament can scrutinize regulations after they have been put in place, the number of regulations being made is such that parliamentary scrutiny is necessarily limited. It is therefore often left to the courts, on application of those affected by a regulation, to determine if the regulation was properly made. Court decisions have determined that even though the powers conferred by the legislation may be broad, a regulation must be authorized. A regulation must fall within the scope or limits of the regulation making powers, not create an offence or tax, and not negate the purpose or a provision of the statute.

The particular roles and functions of certain government members within each House is explored in the chapters on each House.

CHAPTER THREE

Political Parties

Political parties are a necessary reality in the functioning of the Canadian parliamentary system. They are not only important in the electoral system. Much of the structure and work of the House of Commons is based on the fact that political party affiliation of those elected is integral to the determination of the House's makeup. The caucuses of members with the same political affiliation provide stable support for government, provide coordinated opposition, and select the various House officers that allow the business of the House to proceed in an orderly fashion. Funding for research, membership in committees, and participation in the management of the administration for the House is also based on the relative size of each party's caucus.

Development and Entrenchment of Political Parties Within Parliament

Although each Member of Parliament is individually elected and has equal constitutional status and authority, with limited exceptions, members were elected as candidates representing a particular political party. In the United Kingdom, until the late eighteenth to early nineteenth centuries, there were only loose affiliations of members. With the development of responsible government and electoral reform, by the mid-nineteenth century, political parties had become a central feature of political and parliamentary life. Responsible government, combined with the expansion of the vote, accelerated the establishment of political parties. Since the House of Commons was now responsible for who governed, those who wanted to govern sought ways to control the House of Commons.

The best way to obtain the confidence of the House was to try to elect members who would coalesce around an identified agenda and leader. People with similar philosophies, policies, and societal goals would associate with each other. The groups recognized that the best way to achieve their goals was to control the parliamentary agenda by electing as many like-minded candidates as possible. Also, they needed to rally around a leader who would be considered by the monarch for prime minister and be asked to form a government. There were benefits to electors as well, as they were presented with a coordinated platform choice and were able to have a foretaste of the potential government leadership and parliamentary agenda. The establishment of political parties was a means to shape elections and thereby the House of Commons and the resulting government.

Role of Political Parties in Parliament

Following an election, the members elected from the same political party form caucuses within the House of Commons. To be recognized as a caucus and therefore be entitled to the benefits outlined in this section, there needs to be a minimum of twelve members elected from the party in question.

Given that caucuses will generally vote as a block, their relative size will often determine who is called upon by the Governor General to be prime minister and form a government, and who will lead the Opposition. Where one party's caucus represents a majority of seats in the House of Commons, the leader of that party will be called on since it is obvious that they will be able to secure confidence. When no caucus represents a majority of seats, where it can be demonstrated that a combination of caucuses will support a particular leader, that person will be called on to form a government. Otherwise, the leader of the largest caucus will be asked if they are prepared to try to obtain the confidence of the House and govern.

Each caucus meets regularly in private to discuss how they will collectively approach issues in the House and committees. The strategy for supporting or opposing legislation, expected votes, and House assignments will be decided. Caucus will decide who is to sit on what committees, chair committees, and once committees are established, share what is occurring in committee, and strategize on witnesses and other matters. Caucus meetings also provide an opportunity for members to bring constituency and policy concerns to the attention of party leadership, Cabinet ministers, or critics.

Given that each caucus is made up of members from the same political party, it is expected that the caucus will vote as a block on any matter presented to the House of Commons by the government. In many cases votes are "whipped," meaning that members of a caucus are required by their caucus leadership to vote a particular way. Failure to accept a whip will result in discipline, including the possibility of being expelled from caucus. This places the focus on the leaders of each party to indicate what position their caucus will take, from which it is possible to predict support for parliamentary proposals and the outcome of votes.

The smooth running of the House of Commons depends on a degree of cooperation among caucuses. Although political adversaries, each caucus plays a role in the business of the House of Commons, as government supporters, official Opposition, or smaller parties. To allow for business to be conducted smoothly and fairly, each caucus will be represented in the House by two main House officers, in addition to their political leader: the House leader and whip. These three caucus office holders are the main actors that connect the political agenda of the political parties to the caucus and then to the House of Commons. The political, or party, leader is the person who is the face of the party and caucus to the general

population. They are the prime minister, the leader of the Opposition, and the leader of each other caucus (formally referred to as
recognized parties). House leaders are the representatives of the caucuses within the House. They organize the caucus, assigning committee roles to members, organize speaking order on debates, and
negotiate with the House leaders of other caucuses on how matters
will proceed through committees and the House itself. They speak
for the caucus on parliamentary matters, and they stand in for the
party leader when that person is absent from the House. The primary
responsibility of the whips is to make sure that the various members
of the caucus are where they are supposed to be, doing what they
are supposed to be doing, and voting the way that the caucus and
party leadership have decided. Where members are going be absent
or there are other matters that make it difficult for a member to
participate as anticipated, the whip is responsible for resolving the
problem, by finding a substitute or working with opposing whips to
work an appropriate trade-off. Whips are also responsible for disci-
plining members who fail to meet their responsibilities.

Much of the work of the House of Commons, and until recently
the Senate, is organized around the reality of political parties and
their caucuses in each House. The *Parliament of Canada Act* mentions
"party" at least thirty times and sets out additional remuneration to
be paid to the various House officers of "recognized parties."[1] The
rules and practices of the Houses also illustrate the importance of
political parties and their caucuses. The relative amount of time
allocated to each party caucus in debate, the order of speaking, and
the allocation of slots in Question Period are based on the relative sizes of each caucus. The government, along with its supporters, control the agenda of the House, with the official Opposition
being recognized as the next significant block. The other caucuses
are allocated time based on the percentage of seats they have in the
House. Independent members (those not in a recognized caucus)
must depend on agreements with the other parties or the protection
of the Speaker of the House to have a role in the business of the
House and its committees.

As for committees, membership on committees is based on the relative percentage of the number of seats that each caucus has in the House. Therefore, the larger the caucus, the more seats on each committee. The control of committees can have a major impact on what inquiries are held, what witnesses are called, and the content of committee reports. In addition, most committees also follow a pattern of questioning by committee members that is based on the relative number of members. There is no specific number of seats on a committee for independent members, who are often allowed to participate in committee proceedings, but not to vote.

Resourcing Caucuses and Members

To fund each caucus's operations requires resources in personnel and money. Each caucus is provided with funds to run a collective research bureau. Again, the extent of funding is dependent on the relative size of the caucus. The purpose of the funding is to allow each caucus to be prepared for the business of the House by providing up-to-date coverage of the news and other developments, assisting with preparation for Question Period, committee meetings and speeches in the House, and assisting with research as requested. Research bureaus also assist with preparation of caucus meetings and internal communications. Although not required, it is often the caucus chair who is responsible for managing and directing the work of a research bureau.

In addition to research budgets, each of the House officers for a caucus receives additional funds to assist them in carrying out their House duties.

The House of Commons and Senate are independent from the government. This requires each House to be responsible for its own internal management. To provide for appropriate accountability and oversight, each House has its own management board. For the Senate, this is achieved through the Standing Senate Committee on Internal Economy, Budgets and Administration, which is composed of the leader of the government in the Senate (or the government nominee), and the leader of the Opposition in the Senate, or their nominee, and other membership assigned in the usual manner by the Senate. The House of Commons has a Board of Internal Economy, composed of the Speaker, two Cabinet ministers (one of whom is usually the government House leader), the leader of the Opposition (or more often, the Opposition House leader), and other members depending on the number of recognized parties in the House. These bodies are responsible for setting the budgets for their respective House, overseeing the administration that supports the House, and establishing the resources and budget for each caucus, member, and senator, and the rules relating to the use of such budgets. They are also responsible for taking the necessary action against members or senators who are found to have misused resources.

One of the main areas of tension in the use of resources demonstrates that partisanship continues into the House following an election or appointment. It also illustrates the separation between the political and parliamentary functions of members. The spending rules allow members and House officers to use their budgets and resources for partisan, but not political, purposes. This is a real example of the fact that the political philosophies and positions are accepted as a necessary part of the business of the House, and that in many ways the funding reflects this. At the same time, individuals, once elected, become Members of Parliament and are no longer candidates, nor seekers of votes. Resources must be used for their parliamentary functions, not to further their political fortunes. A fine line, but one that is necessary. Once a politician, now a parliamentarian, but always a partisan.

Individuals Participating Through Political Parties

Members of Parliament, ministers, and national party leaders are generally seen as distant and elitist. Individuals feel detached from the government and parliamentarians. The general public see members as politicians who are only focused on them at election time. Individuals may think that all they have is a single vote, and that no one listens to them except to get that vote at elections. This is not the case.

Political parties are a major way for individuals, who are not themselves politicians, to play a role in policy development and remain connected to issues between elections. Virtually all members are elected as representatives of a political party that campaigned on a particular platform. These platforms are developed through party conventions, discussion groups, and input from party members. During meetings, members of the party have the ability to discuss, debate, and develop policies that will form the basis for electoral platforms. Often parties have focused committees based on particular policy issues (e.g., economics, justice, gender issues, or social policy) on which interested party members work to develop initiatives for the party to consider for inclusion in electoral platforms. Since such committees are focused, they may also assist the caucus in responding to developments in Parliament as they emerge between elections.

Individual party members also play a role as sounding boards for Members of Parliament who spend considerable time in Ottawa away from their constituencies. Party members can help identify constituency issues to be addressed by members in the House, in committees, or in communications with government officials. They also meet regularly with the member to discuss the work of Parliament. They can inform a member on how their work, the work of the government, or the Opposition is perceived by individuals, the press, and social groups within the constituency. Members will use this information in caucus discussions and in framing debates in Parliament. For those party members whose candidate was not successful in the election, they can still play a similar role in supporting their party's caucus and members, through meeting with members for neighbouring constituencies and at national levels.

Individual party members are also involved in the selection of candidates to represent the party at elections and in the election of party leaders. Most candidates for election have a long association within a political party, at the local or national level, so that involvement in the party is often a prerequisite for nomination. The selection of candidates is by a vote of all party members in a constituency. The election of leader varies by party. Leadership may be determined by a delegated convention, where each constituency association sends a number of delegates. Leaders may also be selected by direct vote of total party membership or by an indirect vote where each constituency has one vote with the party membership in the constituency determining how the constituency will cast its vote. In all cases, there is a role for individual party members to play both at the constituency and national levels.

CHAPTER FOUR

House of Commons

The House of Commons is the elected House of Parliament. It carries out the constitutional functions of legislating, deliberating, and holding the government to account. It is the body from which the government emanates, and to which the government is continuously accountable. It is also the body in which most legislation, and all legislation relating to taxation and spending, is first introduced, debated, and voted on.

The government ministers sit in the House, and as such are a part of its membership. Those members who form the government remain accountable to the rest of the House. They must answer to the House for all actions that they take as ministers and as a government.

The House of Commons is an assembly composed of its members. As such, its members, as a collective, are the House of Commons. The House of Commons can only act as a collective, and no one member or group of members can be said to speak for the House of Commons. The only way that the House speaks is through its collective votes on bills or resolutions.

Members

Members of the House of Commons are elected for designated constituencies and are known as Members of Parliament, often abbreviated as MPs. They hold this role separately for each Parliament. Once Parliament is dissolved, members cease to be members. They may run again as a candidate in the ensuing election, and if re-elected, they become a member in the next Parliament.

Members of Parliament carry out various constitutional and political functions. They participate in the political and policy discussions within their political party. As a candidate for election, they promote the political platform and leader of their party. Once elected they participate in the business of the House of Commons, which is coordinated by the caucus leadership. A member may also have additional roles as Cabinet minister, parliamentary secretary, shadow Cabinet member, committee member, or committee chair. All the while they will be advocating for constituents, and other interests both inside their constituency and for those whose positions the member may wish to promote. Each member may have a different focus depending on how they perceive their position. Although every member has various roles to play, they also have different interests and goals. Some may want to focus on policy and legislative work, others on parliamentary business such as holding the government to account, promoting partisan positions, and coordinating parliamentary work. Others see the role more from the perspective of representing their community through assisting constituents in accessing and dealing with government departments and seeking to ensure that their constituents come first in all considerations. None of these is the "correct" or "best" role for a Member of Parliament. All are needed for the work of the House as a democratic institution to be done well.

Qualification and Disqualification

The right to be a candidate and be elected a member of the House of Commons is constitutionally protected in Canada. The right to vote and be elected is so fundamental that the notwithstanding clause that allows legislation to be enacted that violates the *Canadian Charter of Rights and Freedoms* (*Charter*) does not apply.[1] These rights can only be limited if such limits are found to be demonstrably justified in a democratic society under section 1 of the *Charter*, and the courts have been particularly vigilant to guard against any unwarranted restrictions. For example, in Canada, the courts have held that there is no justification to restrict prisoner voting.

There are few qualifications and limited exceptions regarding who can be a candidate in a federal election. The starting point is that any citizen 18 years of age or older can run for and be elected a member.

There are, however, a few bases for disqualifications. These fall into three broad categories. First is disqualification based on constitutional conflicts of interest and the requirement of independence of the legislature from the other branches of the state. Second is incapacity such as non-citizenship or incarceration for extended periods of time. Finally, disqualification can be based on the commission of offences related to democracy and the integrity of the electoral process.

In most cases where a person is precluded from voting they are thereby disqualified from being elected. However, the reverse is not true. Disqualification from being a member does not disqualify one from voting.

Although a senator, a member of a legislative assembly, a holder of a federal public office (including public servants), or Crown appointees (including judges) can vote, they cannot hold a seat in the Commons. The reason for most of these restrictions is that the person would be in a conflict of interest if they were a member. In the case of a public office holder, there is a conflict since the House of Commons holds a public servant's employer, the government, to account. In the case of a judge, laws passed by Parliament are subject to judicial interpretation. It is accepted that most public servants can run for office by taking certain types of leave from their job, but if elected they would have to resign from their job.

Members Are Elected for Constituency but Act Collectively as a House of Commons

At present (2022), there are 338 constituencies (formally electoral districts), sometimes referred to as ridings, across Canada. The basis for the overall number of seats is the national census, with any new seats allocated to those provinces with the most growth. At the same time there are some provinces that have a minimum number of seats constitutionally allocated to them so that they have adequate representation in the House of Commons. The population range per constituency is 36,000 to 120,000, with the average just under 105,000. Since constituencies are based on population, in cities constituencies can be geographically small, with rural and scarcely populated areas of the country covering vast land masses.

The number of constituencies and their boundaries is revised every ten years based on census data. There are to be 342 constituencies in 2024, based on the 2021 census. To establish the constituency boundaries, an electoral boundary commission is established to design constituencies that include roughly the same number of constituents. The commissions are politically neutral, so the risk of gerrymandering, or illicitly adjusting constituency boundaries to achieve a political result, is very low.

The configuration of constituencies, along with regional, cultural, and linguistic factors within them, creates a relatively diverse makeup of parliamentarians. The result is that there is a range of viewpoints within each caucus and held by those in Cabinet and Opposition critic positions, which, by convention, are composed of members from each region. Similarly, committees will have mixed interests based on the fact that they are composed of members from all parties. This does not mean that the House of Commons is a perfect reflection of all interests in the country, since each region may have a particular political history that results in most members being elected from the same party, and within each party and community there are various groups that make up the political elite. However, overall, there is a moderate cross-section of interests represented in the House of Commons that reflects the country as a whole.

Although members are elected for a constituency, they are not solely a representative of that constituency. Members obtain the right, through a constituency-based election, to be summoned to the House of Commons. Once summoned, they get their authority from the Constitution, not the electorate. They carry out their role as a member of the House of Commons, not as an agent or representative of the constituency. When they are acting within the House and its committees, members are part of the collective body making a collective decision that has an effect on the entire country.

There are various ways that members will bring the interests of their constituents to the attention of the House throughout the legislating process. They may bring a particular "local" perspective and indicate how a collective decision might have unique effects on the constituency. Constituent views can also be brought to the attention of the House and government through advocacy and accountability functions. However, in the end, members are responsible for being a part of the overall process and for participating in a national forum.

Members are part of a party caucus and have roles assigned to them as supporters either of the government or the Opposition. Caucuses are integral to the functioning of the House of Commons. From the perspective of members, caucus is a venue where they can air their concerns with others, discuss policy and approaches to proceedings, and question the political and parliamentary leadership to determine assignments for proceedings, such as speaking to a bill, and ask questions. Since caucus meetings are held in private, members are able to speak more freely and to explore internal policy and caucus matters without attribution. Once a position has been agreed on, members will often be required to present a common front supporting that position to their constituents, the public, the media, and in proceedings. For those who do not hold House officer positions, committee membership and potential committee chair assignments (or who to support for such positions) is often worked out in caucuses. Some committees and chair positions are seen as more prestigious than others, and assignments can affect the trajectory of a member's parliamentary career. The balance between the "freedom to speak openly" with the potential assignment of parliamentary roles is one that members will likely learn from what goes on behind the closed doors of caucus.

Regardless of their personal views, and those of particular constituents, in the end, the constitutional function of members involves being part of a singular decision-making process of the House resulting in a law that has to operate throughout the country in many different circumstances and contexts.

Members and Constituents

The democratic relationship between members and constituents, and therefore between their constituents and the House of Commons, is not limited to elections. The process of legislating and holding the government to account is an ongoing democratic exercise. Members are the conduit of information between Parliament and their constituency. Members bring matters of concern from their constituency to Parliament. Such concerns may be brought to the appropriate committee, as part of debate, when amending legislation; raised in Question Period or House debates; or made the subject of a member's statement to the House. Members are also responsible for tabling petitions to the government in the House. Through informal channels, members also play the role of intermediary between constituency interests and government departments.

They communicate the decisions taken by Parliament and the government to the constituency. When a member votes in the House they do so as the member for a particular constituency, signifying that the voice of the constituency, through a democratically elected member, has been expressed and registered. Following a decision of the House, the expectation is that the member will communicate the result to constituents. Members are provided with various resources, including a four-times-a-year printed communication to every household in their constituency delivered free by Canada Post, to inform constituents of the member's work and the decisions of the House. No doubt these "householders" are partisan in their perspective; however, the communications must focus on parliamentary and not political work. In this way, the processes and decisions of the House are given democratic legitimacy, and all constituents are able to provide members with feedback.

In addition to their involvement in parliamentary business, which is often partisan, members also play a role akin to that of an ombudsperson for their constituents, which is more focused on assisting individuals rather than on politics. Individuals often ask their Member of Parliament to assist them in accessing government programs and information, or to assist with individual issues and difficulties they are having with government departments. Various ways have been established for individuals to communicate with — and receive communications from — members at no cost. Every member is provided with resources to rent and staff a constituency office to assist constituents. All members have email and other means of electronic communication. One of the privileges enjoyed by members and their constituents is that they can communicate by mail postage free. Any person in Canada can write to a Member of Parliament and mail the letter (without postage) to:

[Name of Member of Parliament]
House of Commons
Ottawa ON K1A 0A6
Canada

Members: Politics and Ethics

Having varied roles and functions, along with the desire to satisfy the interests of their political party, constituents, and supporters, it may seem difficult and daunting for members to avoid confusing what they are doing at any given time. It does not help that the public and the press often confuse politics, partisanship, and parliamentarianism. This is where the various rules for the spending of funds provided to members and the *Conflict of Interest Code for Members of the House of Commons* provide guidelines and systems to assist members in keeping it all straight.[2]

Although members are elected for a specific geographical constituency, and they can act in a partisan fashion while carrying out their parliamentary functions, they are expected generally to act in the overall best interests of the country. They are neither agents nor the pure representatives of anyone. Nor can they be. They may espouse views that are consistent with the political party of which they are a member, those of their constituents, or those of particular groups that have convinced them to support various initiatives. There may be pressures brought to bear by whips and parliamentary leadership, but members cannot be bound in any way to act or vote in a particular fashion. They cannot act for the purpose of advancing the interests of a third party, family members, or themselves. They cannot accept money or favours for advancing such interests, nor can they enter into an agreement to be bound to a particular position. Where there is a potential for a matter to be dealt with that would have the effect of providing a particular benefit to a member or their family, they are expected to disclose the interest and remove themselves from participating in the debates or votes on the matter.

Any of these activities can be the subject of an investigation by the ethics commissioner for potential violation of the *Conflict of Interest Code for Members of the House of Commons* that forms part of the standing orders of the House. If a member is found to have violated the *Code*, the violation will be made public (which may have political consequences) and they can be disciplined by their caucus and the House of Commons.

To provide transparency, people who seek to influence members, other than constituents and community groups, must register as lobbyists and disclose all meetings they have with members. Members also have an obligation to track meetings with lobbyists. In the case of a serious breach of these rules, both the member and the third party may be charged criminally under the bribery of public officials provisions of the *Criminal Code*.[3]

While it may be difficult to draw, there is a line between acting in a partisan manner or in the interests of one's constituents and acting for the purpose of benefiting an individual, business, family member, or oneself. There are also lines between lobbying, advocating, and bribery. Ultimately, if the focus of members remains on the public good, rather than a benefit to particular persons, members are free to fearlessly pursue their agendas and carry out their parliamentary business, no matter how partisan their words and actions may be.

The distinction that can cause some difficulty for members is that they can act and use House resources for reasons that may be partisan, but not for those that are political. This confusion can be resolved not by looking at how activities are carried out, but rather looking at the activity itself. Is the activity for which the resources are being used part of a parliamentary function? Or is it political? Or is it personal? Only those that meet the test of being parliamentary can benefit from the use of parliamentary resources, including funds, staff, and office space.

There are some activities that might fall close to the ethical line, particularly when members are serving as "ombudsperson" for constituents, or meeting constituents to communicate what the member, and the caucus in which they sit, plans to do in Parliament. Some may see this as political rather than parliamentary activity, but it is not. If the right "test" is applied, the issue can be easily answered. Is the purpose to help or discuss, or is the purpose to seek votes, raise funds, or give a platform to a political party? No doubt helping constituents and keeping them informed may assist the member as a candidate in future elections, but that cannot be the purpose for the use of resources. To assist members in making these determinations, the Board of Internal Economy, composed of members from each caucus, has established rules and guidelines and can make necessary determinations that define and police these distinctions.

Members wear many hats. They are members of political parties. They have been elected and are likely to run as candidates in subsequent elections. As a result, political considerations with a view to the next election is a normal inclination. But as an elected Member of Parliament, each wears the hat of a parliamentarian, albeit the colour of their political team. To avoid running afoul of the ethics rules and the rules relating to spending, members must remember that in the House, and when assisting constituents, they are playing the parliamentary, not the political game; even though political games also may be being played at the same time. The funds and benefits they receive as a member are to be used only to carry out their parliamentary functions, not their political ones. Knowing what one is doing and why is crucial in this context.

Organization of the House of Commons

The House of Commons is organized along party lines. The chamber is set out in a rectangle with ranks of benches, with desks for members arranged down each of the long sides. At one end, in the centre of the aisle separating the benches, sits the Speaker on a raised dais. The caucus of the party of the prime minister sits in the seats to the Speaker's right. The prime minister sits in the middle seat in the front bench. The Cabinet ministers sit in the front row and in the second row spreading out from immediately behind the prime minster. Opposite the prime minister sits the leader of the Opposition, with the Opposition critics and members arranged similarly opposite the ministers and the caucus that supports the government. Depending on the size of the caucuses of other parties, they will sit in blocks of seats, mostly on the Opposition side of the House. This configuration symbolizes and enhances the concept and structure of government and opposition inherent in the Westminster system of government.

The Speaker

The House of Commons is presided over by the Speaker. The Speaker is elected by the members at the beginning of each Parliament and holds that office until the next Speaker is chosen at the beginning of the next Parliament (a Speaker can be re-elected). The term Speaker refers to the person who speaks on behalf of the House, particularly to the Senate and to the Queen as represented by the Governor General. They are the public face of the House of Commons. When they speak or act outside of the proceedings of the House, they are scrupulously neutral. They only convey what the House has given them authority to say, not what they may personally believe or know. This protects both the Speaker and the House. The Speaker is also responsible for ensuring that the privileges of the House and its members are respected and protected, both inside and outside proceedings.

The most public role of the Speaker is as presiding officer of the House of Commons. In this role they work to ensure orderly debate, that all members are respected, and that their privileges within debates are protected. The Speaker is neutral and respects any decision taken by the House. Therefore, the Speaker only votes when there is a tie. Although they can vote as they choose, convention and tradition provide that the Speaker will vote to sustain the existing position, for example, they will vote to continue debate, to not pass legislation, and to retain confidence in the government. When a question of privilege arises, the Speaker does not determine whether privilege has been breached, since that decision can only be made by the House as a whole. The Speaker will listen to each side of the issue and determine whether a plausibly arguable case has been made for the matter to be dealt with by the House, usually following consideration by the committee responsible for privileges and proceedings.

Caucuses

As discussed in Chapter 3, political parties have been a feature of Canadian politics since before Confederation. This reality is clearly reflected in the structure of the House of Commons, as well as in its operation. Pursuant to the *Parliament of Canada Act*[4] and the Standing Orders of the House of Commons, each caucus of twelve or more members elected from the same political party is considered a "recognized party" within the House. The significance of obtaining recognized party status should not be underestimated. As a "recognized party" a caucus will receive proportionate representation on committees, have a place in the rotation of questions and speakers in House proceedings, be consulted when the Standing Orders or legislation requires that the leaders of recognized parties be consulted, and the caucus will receive funding for research and caucus support. This support allows members to better prepare and coordinate themselves for questions, debates, and participation in the House and committees. Those members who are not part of a recognized party caucus are considered independent members. Even when members are elected as representative of a political party, if that party does hold twelve seats in the House, they are considered independent members. They may be able to attend committees, but may not participate as full voting members, they must rely on the Speaker to be added to the list of questioners or speakers, and they must rely on their own staff to prepare for participation. While the Speaker will try to include independent members in proceedings, the recognized parties in the House and the Standing Orders can make it difficult.

Each caucus is similarly structured regarding the workings of the House. There is a party leader, who may be the prime minister or the leader of the Opposition. In addition, each caucus will have a House leader who organizes the caucus within the House, assigns lists of questioners and speakers, and will speak for the caucus in the House. House leaders often consult with each other to manage the business of the House and will represent their caucus on the Board of Internal Economy, which is responsible for the administration of the House of Commons and the allocation and oversight of resources provided to members and caucuses to carry out their parliamentary functions. Each caucus will also have a whip who is responsible for ensuring that members are where they are supposed to be, particularly when there are votes or major debates. Whips are also responsible for dealing with the personal issues of members, resolving issues involving members, and imposing discipline on members when it might be required.

House Administration

As indicated earlier, the House of Commons is not a government department, nor part of the executive. It is responsible for its own financial management, human resources, and internal policies. As a result, the House of Commons has a relatively large administration that supports members and the House in conducting their business. It has three major support functions. First, it supports the parliamentary business in both the House and committees. For example, clerks support the Speaker in the House by keeping records, recording votes, and providing assistance with applying the rules. They also keep the records of the House, including agendas, journals, and *Hansard* (a record of debates). They carry out a similar role with committees, but with the added responsibility of arranging meetings, and securing the attendance of witnesses. Second, the administration supports members, by providing office space, security, and assisting in the administration of the funds and resources provided to members. This can include keeping track of spending, providing technical support, providing advice on the application of rules for member spending, and advice on human resource matters. Finally, since the House of Commons is separate from the government, it is responsible for its own administration. It has to manage its own staff, contracting, information technology, and other facets of administration.

To manage these administrative and financial functions, the House of Commons has its own internal management structure, overseen by the Board of Internal Economy. The board has a membership composed of members from each recognized party based on the percentage of seats in the House of Commons. The board is chaired by the Speaker, has at least two Cabinet ministers, and usually at least the House leader of each party. Through its bylaws and policies, the board sets the general policy and budget for the House administration, but has assigned the day-to-day management of the administration to the clerk and a management team of senior employees of the House. The board is also responsible for establishing a budget and policy for expenditures for all members, caucuses, and House officers. Assisted by the House administration, the board has exclusive jurisdiction to determine whether any expenditure or proposed expenditure is properly made for carrying out parliamentary functions in accordance with its policies. Since the use of resources can determine how a member carries out their functions, any interference with the decisions of the board would be an interference with the House of Commons and a breach of parliamentary privilege.

The Clerk and House Officials

The clerk of the House of Commons is the most senior House official. They are appointed by the government on the advice of the House of Commons, and they continue in their role from Parliament to Parliament. They have two major functions. Their primary responsibility is to ensure that the House functions properly and that the business of the House is accurately recorded. They are responsible for keeping the records and journals of the House of Commons, advising the Speaker on questions of parliamentary privilege, and swearing in members and ensuring that members also receive advice and assistance in all procedural matters. In addition to their parliamentary functions, the clerk is the person responsible for the administration of the House, both in support of members and the chamber and for the House administration itself.

The clerk is supported in this role by various senior House officials, two of particular note. One is the sergeant-at-arms. There has been a sergeant-at-arms for the House of Commons in England and the United Kingdom since 1415, and in Canada since before Confederation. Their role has historically focused on the provision of security and management of the physical space occupied by the House of Commons and its members. They are also responsible for the security of the mace, as the symbol of the Queen within Parliament. With the passage of time, and the need to modernize the operations of the House of Commons, many of the administrative roles of the clerk and sergeant-at-arms are now shared with other senior managers. The other House official of note is the law clerk and parliamentary counsel. They provide independent legal advice to the Speaker, members, and the administration. They are also responsible for ensuring the bills introduced, and amendments proposed, will fit with the procedures of the House and result in legislation in proper form.

Functions of the House of Commons

The House of Commons has two primary functions — accountability and legislating. When carrying out its accountability function, the House acts alone. When carrying out its legislating function it acts as a part of Parliament. In addition to these primary functions, the House of Commons can make inquiries into any matter that falls within its legislative competencies, has responsibility for approving the appointment of some officers of Parliament, and is a forum for expressing national concerns.

Confidence, Legitimacy, and Accountability

As the confidence chamber, the House of Commons plays a fundamental role in determining who will form the government. Following a general election, the person who is believed to have the confidence of the House of Commons, that is, the person who is most likely to be able to get a majority vote on their proposed agenda, is invited by the Governor General to form a government as prime minister. The prime minister in turn will select Members of Parliament (and exceptionally senators) to be ministers within the Cabinet. As Members of Parliament, they participate in the business of the House in a dual capacity. As members, ministers have all the same rights, privileges, and responsibilities as all Members of Parliament. They also have the additional responsibility of being accountable for the matters entrusted to them as minister, and have collective responsibility, along with all ministers, for the actions of the government.

For most ministers, a parliamentary secretary is also appointed. The role of the parliamentary secretary is to act as a liaison between the House of Commons and the minister. Since ministers are often absent from the House to conduct government business, their parliamentary secretary stands in for the minister in the House and may be called on to answer questions or take the place of the minister in the House.

The requirement that the government has and retains the confidence of the House of Commons determines who is to govern and for how long. It gives legitimacy to the actions of the prime minister and the government. At all times that the government has the confidence of the House of Commons it is presumed that the government has the support of a majority of the Members of Parliament, and that it is therefore acting on behalf of the people of the country with the support of their Members of Parliament. Once confidence is lost, the legitimacy of the government to speak and act as if it has the support of the country can no longer be assumed.

If the government loses the confidence of the House of Commons, the prime minister, and therefore the government, must either resign or the prime minister will request that Parliament be dissolved and an election be called to establish the House of Commons for the next Parliament.

Once Parliament is dissolved, the House of Commons ceases to exist, and all Members of Parliament cease to be members. To maintain governmental operations and necessary decision making, the government and ministers stay in place on an interim basis and govern pursuant to the caretaker convention until after the election.

Because the government must always retain the confidence of the House of Commons, it is perpetually accountable to it. Various proceedings and procedures of the House of Commons are designed to allow it to hold the government to account. The Opposition in the House leads in the accountability, but all non-minister members also have this responsibility. However, in the case of those who are in the same caucus as the ministers, the accountability is tempered by party discipline and therefore usually takes place in caucus meetings rather than openly on the floor of the House.

Accountability factors into many forms of proceedings. The most obvious and public is oral questions, known popularly as Question Period. Each day the House sits, a period of time is allocated to Question Period, which allows members to put questions to the government on any matter for which the government is responsible. Since Question Period is time limited and given public prominence, all members would like to participate, but the list of proposed questioners provided to the Speaker is controlled by the party leadership. This control is also a way for the party to keep control of their caucus members, by either coordinating questions or not listing members who deviate from the party line.

The format of short questions and responses with the prime minister being confronted by the leader of the Opposition provides a glimpse into the political issues of the day, the focus of criticism, the government's immediate response, and how each of the leaders presents themselves in pressure situations. Clips of Question Period are often used in newscasts, blogs, and other media. Each day that the House of Commons sits, forty-five minutes are given to oral questions. Except for ministers and parliamentary secretaries, members pose questions to the prime minister and ministers. Questioners have a short period to preface and ask questions, and ministers are expected to provide a response within a slightly longer timeframe. The first questions are normally posed by the leader of the Opposition and generally they are posed to the prime minister when they are present. It is expected that when the prime minister and ministers are in Ottawa, they will attend Question Period to face the Opposition. While questions from the government backbench are often softer than those of the Opposition, Question Period is an opportunity for members to raise constituent concerns.

Since Question Period forms part of the parliamentary proceedings there are some loose boundaries on the scope of questions that can be posed. Questions must fall within the functions of Parliament. They must have some connection to federal legislative capacity, or the functioning of the federal government and its agencies. Careful crafting can have the effect of stretching the boundaries, if there is some political capital to be gained. For example, a direct question could not be asked relating to hospital staffing since this would fall within provincial jurisdiction. However, a question could be asked of the minister responsible for federal transfer of funds for health care regarding what level of staffing they would expect provinces to have given the level of funds transferred. Questions of a personal nature are generally off-limits; however, a minister's fitness to hold a particular office, or the effects on performance, if carefully worded, are within bounds. When dealing with matters that are more personal, the Opposition must be careful to avoid appearing as bullies targeting an individual as a person rather than as minister. The line can often blur as the Opposition seeks to demonstrate ministerial "incompetence" or "scandal" with the objective of forcing a minister to resign or the prime minister to act to remove or shuffle the minister to another ministry. The results can be extremely embarrassing for a government and may become election issues. Even without such dramatic consequences, the embarrassments from prolonged questioning can involve considerable deflection of the government's focus away from its legislative and policy agenda.

Although Question Period is the most visible and boisterous form of accountability, its format and publicity mean that it sometimes becomes more political theatre than a forum for explanation and dialogue, which is one of the main hallmarks of true accountability. Question Period may not always advance parliamentary and government accountability, but it feeds into the ultimate form of accountability — elections. The Opposition can use this opportunity to raise issues that may embarrass the government, provide grist for press-based publicity, and attempt to focus the next election on the Opposition's attacks and the government's defence of its performance.

An expanded form of questioning is through the process of written questions, or questions on the order paper. These are questions in writing by members that are filed with the clerk's office. They are addressed to the government, which is required to file a written response, which is tabled in the House. Both the question and response are recorded in the journals of the House. These questions usually require more detailed and lengthier responses relating to government operations and spending. Another form of written inquiry can result from the tabling of petitions by members. Where a petition tabled has a minimum number of signatures, the government is required to table a response.

The procedural rules of the House, known as the Standing Orders, allow the government to set the agenda and the schedule for most of debate time. However, there are specific rules that allow the Opposition to determine the business of the House. A set number of days must be set aside as supply days, commonly referred to as Opposition days. As the name suggests, the Opposition is able to set the general business of the House for those days. This gives the Opposition the ability to debate the topic of its choice, often designed to expose the government to criticism, either directly or indirectly. There is also specific time established for the Opposition to debate the program of the government as set out in the Speech from the Throne, and for debate on the budget.

At the end of each sitting day during adjournment proceedings, members, usually from the Opposition, also have the opportunity to seek further information on up to three topics relating to matters raised in Question Period or on any written question for which a reply has not been received within the prescribed time. If a member can convince the Speaker that there is a matter that constitutes an emergency, the Speaker can allow a longer time for the adjournment debate on the matter giving rise to the emergency.

Committees

The House has various standing committees, some that focus on both legislation and accountability, and some that focus primarily on accountability. Five of those most focused on accountability are chaired by a member of the official Opposition: public accounts; access to information, privacy, and ethics; government operations and estimates; status of women; and the joint committee for the scrutiny of regulations. These committees also have one fewer government member so that when voting, the opposition parties have an advantage.

Since committees have a focused mandate, they can concentrate their efforts and probe more effectively into aspects of government activities, policies, and legislation. Committees are also able to set their own agendas and schedule their work, subject to time limits to report contained in the Standing Orders or in references to the committee. Committees are also given the power to "send for persons, papers and records," which means they call witnesses and can require that documents and records be provided to the committee as evidence.[5] This process allows committees to conduct in-depth inquiries and studies.

If a witness indicates that they are concerned that they may be subject to reprisals, or that they may be exposing themselves to some form of legal consequence, they will be reassured by the committee that witnesses have the same protection of the privileges of the House that members have. Whatever a witness says or provides to a committee cannot be used in any legal proceeding or investigation and cannot form the basis for reprisals. Although the House has the ability to find an untruthful or reluctant witness in contempt and punish them, it also has the ability and responsibility to protect witnesses from reprisals within government and from the courts. This balance encourages witnesses to come forward and provide truthful and full testimony.

Once a committee has completed a study, it generally prepares a report to the House. Reports will set out the various findings of the committee and may make recommendations for action by the House or the government. Once adopted, the recommendations effectively become orders of the House. Where a committee makes a request of the government, or asks the government to take some action, a deadline is set for the government to provide a response to the committee by way of tabling a response in the House.

Officers of Parliament

Government activities are complex and varied. As a result, it is difficult for Parliament and its committees to provide the necessary ongoing, in-depth, and systematic review and oversight of all government activities. Also, there are certain expectations of government activities and programs that are common to all departments and agencies, such that it is difficult for Parliament to ensure that common standards are adhered to through individual ministerial accountability to Parliament. Therefore, Parliament has created various "officers of Parliament" to assist in its oversight role. Officers of Parliament are individuals given a statutory mandate to oversee a particular aspect of government activity and report their findings and recommendations directly to Parliament, rather than to a minister or through a minister to Parliament.

The longest-standing and most well-known officer of Parliament is the Auditor General. Other officers of Parliament include the Ethics Commissioner, the Privacy Commissioner, the Information Commissioner, the Chief Electoral Officer, and the Official Languages Commissioner. The mandate of each is such as to allow for oversight of government activities free from government interference. By reporting to Parliament, the reports are not screened or edited by the government. Nor is the timing of the report within the control of the government.

A more recent creation of Parliament is the Parliamentary Budget Officer to provide independent analysis to Parliament of proposed government spending, budget estimates, and the cost and effects of proposed programs and taxes. This office allows Parliament to have a neutral assessment free of government "spin." In addition to these mandated responsibilities, individual members can also ask for information and opinions on various proposed spending and costs.

Particular Significant Debates

There are two particular debates during which the House of Commons has an opportunity to consider the overall program and proposals of the government: the address in reply to the Speech from the Throne and the budget. The Standing Orders of the House set out specific periods for these debates, and if the motion to agree to either the Speech from the Throne or the Budget is defeated it is considered that the government no longer has the confidence of the House. In all cases if a vote on the Speech from the Throne is lost, except when the Speech from the Throne is the first of a Parliament, the prime minister will request that Parliament be dissolved and an election held.

The Speech from the Throne is delivered by the Governor General in the Senate with the members of the House of Commons also present. Although titled the Speech from the Throne and delivered by the Governor General, the speech is prepared by the Prime Minister's Office. A Speech from the Throne is delivered at the opening of each session of a Parliament. The speech sets out the general program of the government and broadly outlines the legislative agenda of the government, thus indicating what the government expects of Parliament in the session in which the speech is delivered.

Once delivered, the speech is sent to the House of Commons to be debated and voted on. Except for a *pro forma* bill that is introduced to claim various privileges, generally no legislative business is concluded by the House of Commons until the motion on the speech has been passed. Agreeing to the motion on the speech does not necessarily mean that the House of Commons will agree to the legislation foreshadowed by the speech. The government will still have to introduce and pass each piece of legislation in due course.

The second major debate provided for concerns the budget. It is usual for the minister of finance, on behalf of the government, to deliver a budget annually, usually in mid- to late spring. The budget normally sets out the general state of the economy and projections of revenues, expenses, and deficits or surpluses for the next year and the following few years. The budget also outlines the various tax and fiscal policies of the government, which will form the basis for the necessary legislation. The budget motion is set out in the Standing Orders as "That this House approve in general the budgetary policy of the government." Like the vote on the Speech from the Throne, the vote is of general approval. To implement the various measures required by the budget, the government will introduce one or more budget implementation bills that are subject to amendment and votes that are likely to also be considered matters of confidence, since they deal with supply — that is, with the money the government needs.

Legislating

The largest amount of time spent by the House of Commons is in legislating. It is the activity that most people associate with Parliament, and the House of Commons in particular. It is the activity that affects people directly. Parliament is the only entity that can impose any form of taxation and authorize any spending of public money. It is the only institution that is specifically authorized by the Constitution to make laws. At the federal level this includes the power to legislate with respect to criminal law and to impose both direct and indirect taxes.

Constitutional Limits

As discussed in Chapter 1, Canada is a federal state in which the power to legislate is divided between the federal Parliament and provincial legislatures. As a result, neither level of legislature has full legislative sovereignty, but together they do. The *Constitution Act, 1867*[6] sets out various matters that fall within the jurisdiction of Parliament or provincial legislatures. As a result, the legislative authority of Parliament is restricted to those matters assigned to Parliament by the Constitution. Another way to put it is to say that the legislative capacity of Parliament is limited by the constitutional legislative authority assigned to provincial legislatures.

In 1982, the Constitution was amended to, among other provisions, add a series of constitutional rights and freedoms. Most of these are found in the *Canadian Charter of Rights and Freedoms*.[7] A second part of the *Constitution Act, 1982* protects Aboriginal and treaty rights.[8] The effect of these rights and freedoms is to further restrict the legislative capacity and sovereignty of Parliament. However, many of the rights and freedoms can be specifically overridden for a period of up to five years and are subject to such reasonable limits, in written laws, that are demonstrably justified. Not only does the Constitution place an obligation on Parliament to respect the rights and freedoms, but it also allows Parliament to balance and limit those rights and freedoms against public interests where it can demonstrate the reasonableness of the limits. This responsibility has had an impact on the content, practices, and procedures of both Houses of Parliament.

Money Bills

Although most bills may be first presented in either House, the *Constitution Act, 1867* requires that all bills that include provisions for the spending of public money, or that impose any tax or duty, first be presented in the House of Commons. In addition, any bill that appropriates funds requires a Royal Recommendation, which is a message from the Governor General recommending the bill to the House. Since the Governor General, by convention, only acts on the advice of the Cabinet, this means that any bill that spends funds must have the approval of Cabinet before it can be introduced in the House of Commons. The government, therefore, has complete control over the introduction of any and all bills that involve spending or taxes. Changes to a bill that would increase spending or taxes, or that change any condition or qualifications that would have the effect of increasing expenditures needs to have a new Royal Recommendation. The requirement for a Royal

Recommendation allows the government to restrict the scope of private members' bills (bills introduced by non-ministers), amendments in committee, and bills that originate in the Senate. In any of these situations, if the amendment or bill would, if introduced by the government, require a Royal Recommendation, the government can stop the amendment or bill from being voted on by not seeking the recommendation.

Types of Bills

There are three types of bills: government bills, private members' bills, and private bills.

Government bills, sometimes referred to as public bills, are those introduced by government ministers and can cover any matter over which the federal Parliament has jurisdiction. They are drafted by lawyers in the Department of Justice, on direction of the Cabinet, which has been fully briefed by the various government departments sponsoring and affected by the legislation. Since the government has the ability to seek Royal Recommendations, it can propose all manner of policy, taxation, and spending when presenting bills to the House of Commons. Government bills are given priority in the House, with a large percentage of House time, procedures, and resources dedicated to government business. The order in which government business is proceeded with is determined by the government House leader.

Private members' bills are bills that are introduced by private members (non-ministers) and can deal with any subject matter within the jurisdiction of Parliament. But, because of the restrictions imposed by the requirement for Royal Recommendation for any bill that involves the spending of money, their scope is severely limited, unless there is government support (which is extremely rare). These bills are drafted by, or with the assistance of, lawyers at the House of Commons on instruction from the member introducing the bill. Although a member may place a bill on the order paper of the House at any time, the bills are proceeded with in a particular order, determined by the House. Because of the large number of members, the limited time afforded to private members' business in the House, and the limited staff of the House, there are special processes in place to allocate House time and resources to manage private members' business. At the beginning of a Parliament, and periodically when necessary to replenish the list, a lottery is held that orders all private members into a list for the debate of private members' business (either a bill or motion). House resources for private members' bills are also allocated based on the list (for example, the order in which lawyers draft private members' bills). To ensure that private members' bills are not likely to be ruled out of order on the basis of jurisdiction or the need for Royal Recommendation, they are vetted by a committee dedicated to private members' business, to advise members and the House on these issues. Finally, there is limited time given to discussion of private members' business, and if time runs out on debate of the bill at early stages, the bill is dropped. As a result, few private members' bills become law. Notwithstanding this fact, they play a political role in allowing every member to raise and discuss issues that they believe are necessary to bring to the attention of the public and the government through a parliamentary debate.

Private bills are bills that affect a particular institution that has been established by an earlier Act, or that for some reason requires institutional-specific legislation. These include certain universities, churches, and charities established prior to the enactment of generalized public legislation regulating such bodies.

Legislating Process

All bills, to become law, must be passed through three readings (votes) in each House. Although there are some "short-cuts" where there is consent of all members, or deemed consent in the Standing Orders, each bill in the House of Commons passes through the following steps: introduction and first reading, second reading and referral to committee, committee hearings and study, committee report to the House, and third reading. The bill is then sent to the Senate where it will go through similar steps and three readings. If a bill was first introduced in the Senate (and passes through the three readings in the Senate), it is received from the Senate and will go through the three steps of the House as outlined.

All bills are identified by a number as they go through the legislative process, with the numbering restarted with each session of Parliament. As a result, many bills will have the same number. It is therefore best, particularly once a bill is passed and enacted, to use the name of the legislation rather than continuing to refer to the substance as "Bill C-xx." (Bills beginning with C are those first introduced in the House of Commons; those beginning with S were first introduced in the Senate.)

First reading of a bill is short and there is no debate. The member introducing the bill will provide a short introduction about what the bill is about. The Standing Orders then provide that the bill is to be deemed to have been read a first time and sent to be printed. The second reading is the main debate on the principles and substance of the bill. The member introducing the bill and the main Opposition critic lead the debate and have extended time to make their speeches. The debate continues until all members who wish to speak to the bill have done so, or there is a motion to end debate. A vote on second reading will then take place, and, if passed, the bill is referred to the appropriate committee of the House for closer study.

Once the committee has sufficient evidence it will begin clause-by-clause consideration of the bill, which is a section-by-section review. During this process, the members of the committee will propose various amendments to the bill. Each amendment, and each clause of the bill (with or without amendment) is voted on by the committee.

Although not subject to a formal whip, as may be the case for votes in the House, the work of committees is carefully watched and managed by each party's whip. As legislation is usually proposed to advance the government's agenda, the government seeks to ensure that any proposed and agreed to amendment both meets the purpose of the legislation and is consistent with the overall government agenda.

The committee prepares a report of its proceedings, including any amendments that have been agreed upon. The House then considers the report at what is referred to as report stage. Any proposed amendments are debated and voted on. Once the various amendments are dealt with, the bill is then debated at third reading, with short wrap-up speeches followed by a final vote.

After the vote on third reading approves a bill, it is sent to the Senate for its consideration. The House will only become further involved with the bill if it is returned from the Senate with proposed amendments. The House will then consider the proposals, and if the amendments are agreed to, the bill will be sent for royal assent. If the amendments are not approved, the bill will then pass between the House and the Senate until a single text is agreed to.

CHAPTER FIVE

Senate

Background and Overview

Like many countries, Canada has a national Parliament that is bicameral. It has two legislative and debating chambers, the House of Commons and the Senate. The House of Commons is elected and is the assembly of which the government must retain the confidence, and in which the prime minister and the vast majority of minsters sit. On the other hand, senators are appointed on the recommendation of the prime minister and sit until the age of 75. As a result, many dismiss the Senate as not necessary because it is not democratic and not subject to the same level of public scrutiny and accountability. There are frequent calls to either change the Senate so that it is elected or to abolish it. Despite a 2014 Supreme Court of Canada decision that indicates that such changes would require difficult constitutional amendments, calls for reform continue. Even when the desire for constitutional reform is muted, there is a sense in the public that the Senate is anachronistic and irrelevant. What is clear from this is that the Senate and its role are misunderstood and undervalued.

The Senate makes various important contributions to Parliament, and Canada is better for it. Its function is often referred to as a chamber of sober second thought, and this is not far from the truth. Although careful examination of bills passed in the House is not the Senate's only function, it is a primary one. Despite being separate and distinct from the House of Commons, much of its work is inextricably tied to that of the Commons.

Independence of Senators

Not only is the work of the Senate institutionally separate from that of the House of Commons, each senator enjoys an independence that comes from how they obtain their office. Senators are appointed by the Governor General on the advice of the prime minister. They are appointed, and hold their office, until age 75. As a result, although they are appointed on the recommendation of a prime minister who leads a particular political party, senators are not beholden to that prime minister, nor to that party, for their continued ability to carry out their constitutional functions as a senator. They do not depend on the party or its leader for electoral support in elections, since senators do not have to run in elections. They also do not have to accept a party's whip to retain favour within the party or the House. Failure to vote the way a particular party wants has limited consequences.

Until 2015, however, there was an assumption that senators owed allegiance to the party caucus of the prime minister that recommended their appointment. Often appointments to the Senate were made based on political connections, with numerous senators having been former ministers, former Members of Parliament, or party stalwarts and loyal party members that would form caucuses within the Senate along party lines. These caucuses would then be funded or provided with committee opportunities and the benefit of some form of precedence within the Senate based on party strength within the Senate. It was not uncommon for senators and Members of Parliament from the same party to caucus together. Depending on how long a government was in power, a prime minister could effectively stack the Senate with party adherents for the foreseeable future. So, when there was a change of government following an election, there was a good possibility that the majority in the Senate was opposite to that in the House of Commons. This had been the pattern from the time of Confederation.

In January 2014, then Liberal leader Justin Trudeau expelled all Liberal senators from the Liberal caucus, causing the Liberal senators to become independent senators. Following the 2015 election, now Prime Minister Trudeau set up a process for appointing senators who were expected to be more independent of political parties. This has resulted in Senate appointments being better able to address the concern that various groups are unrepresented or underrepresented within the House of Commons. At the time of writing (Fall 2021), more than half of the senators are independent.

For internal working and support within the Senate, senators have formed loose caucus arrangements, known as groups, with like-minded senators. At the beginning of the 44th Parliament, in late 2021, a bill was introduced in the Senate to amend the *Parliament of Canada Act*[1] to recognize the movement away from party caucuses to the new reality of groups. These changes are likely to be reflected in the Rules of the Senate of Canada, including committee assignments. Financial and administrative support will also be aligned with the new reality. Whether these reforms to the Senate become the norm will only be evident once there is an election that results in a different prime minister.

Intent and Purpose for the Senate

This new appointment process is somewhat in keeping with the original intent and purpose of the Senate to be a check on an elected assembly, which is based on population, with concentrations of population in certain geographic parts of the country. During the Confederation debates, considerable time was spent on the upper house, which was to become the Senate. It was always intended that there be a bicameral Parliament, but the structure and purpose was less certain. There was no defined class system that was the basis for the House of Lords in the UK Parliament. There were linguistic and religious divides, and there was a concern that the population in Ontario, which was predominantly English-speaking and Protestant, would overtake that of Quebec (which was predominantly French-speaking and Catholic) and the Maritime provinces. There was also some concern with how to approach the potential expansion of Canada to the west and north. Finally, there was concern that the provincial governments and local interests would be swallowed up by a larger and more powerful federal government. The solution was to create a Senate that had equal representation by region, with Ontario, Quebec, and the Maritime provinces (originally Nova Scotia and New Brunswick) each having one-third of the seats in the Senate. This way, regional interests with their unique cultural, linguistic, and religious makeup, would be represented in one of the Houses of Parliament and be able to act as a counterbalance to the majority-based, partisan House of Commons. As Canada expanded, the Senate also grew by adding seats for the region of the west, seats for the north, and additional seats for newly added Atlantic provinces. But the balance was maintained with equal representation for Ontario, Quebec, the Western provinces, and the Atlantic provinces, with additional seats for the northern territories.

While the regional makeup of the Senate was set out in the Constitution Acts, strengthened provincial governments have resulted in provinces directly protecting their own interests through federal-provincial meetings of premiers and the prime minister, and provincial ministerial counterparts meeting together and with relevant federal Cabinet ministers. This has resulted in the Senate not formally focusing on provincial or regional matters and has resulted in other interests being the focus of the work of senators.

While no longer resulting from an overtly political process, most new appointments usually fall within the broad political philosophy of the prime minister. The shift from party representation in Senate appointments has accelerated a refocusing of the purpose of the Senate away from regional representation to "rights" protection. The new appointment process allows for bringing individuals who do not have formal political ties into Parliament to fill obvious gaps of underrepresented and marginalized groups absent from membership in the House of Commons. This process, if continued, will likely see the development of groups of senators that seek to ensure that rights and interests of groups, such as Indigenous peoples, women, and others, are protected and promoted. At Confederation, the role of the Senate was to ensure that provincial constitutional rights were protected, or at least considered, in the face of the political expediency of the House of Commons. Today the role of the Senate is still to ensure that constitutional and other rights are not unduly compromised in the legislative and parliamentary process. However, the rights that are of concern have changed. The Senate, as a review body of second thought, is still needed and best suited to focus its efforts to protect the interests that might have been overlooked or neglected in the House of Commons.

What appeared to be an institution that was anachronistic, irrelevant, and out of touch, and a sinecure for has-been political hacks, seems to be seeing a revitalization through a revised appointment process that allows it to refocus on its original purposes. The combination of "life-time" tenure, formal disconnection from traditional political parties, and appointments to address underrepresentation should allow the Senate to better carry out its constitutional functions, and its purpose to protect "minority" rights, in a twenty-first century context.

The Senate Chamber

The Senate has a physical design similar to the House of Commons. There are two sets of desks arranged in rows down the length of the chamber, separated by an aisle. The Speaker sits at one end on a raised dais, with a clerk's table in front of the Speaker's chair. When the Senate is sitting, a mace is placed on the table with the crown pointing toward the Speaker's right. The atmosphere of debate in the Senate is somewhat less acrimonious and lacks some of the political theatre that is found in the elected House of Commons. There are fewer time limits on debate and interventions may appear to be more courteous. The role of the Speaker is also a bit different. The Speaker may leave the chair to a deputy in order to speak in debates and may also vote in Senate business.

In addition to the day-to-day business of the Senate, the Senate chamber is the location where the entire Parliament meets, primarily for the reading of the Speech from the Throne by the Governor General, and the granting of royal assent. At the beginning of each Parliament and session of Parliament, the House of Commons is summoned to the Senate Chamber to attend the Governor General and the Senate to hear the speech. Similarly, from time to time the House will be summoned to attend in the Senate chamber when in-person royal assent to bills is being given by the Governor General or their designate.

The Functions of the Senate

Conscience of Parliament

Constitutionally, the Senate has similar powers to those of the House of Commons. It is a complete House of Parliament and has the same capacity to legislate and carry out accountability functions. There are, however, two significant distinctions. All bills involving the expenditure of money or taxation must first be introduced in the House of Commons, and the government does not need the confidence of the Senate to govern. Most types of bills can therefore originate in the Senate, and the Senate and its committees regularly inquire into the business and operations of government and make decisions relating to their findings that have political fallout, or call for changes in government operations and policy. The Senate has the capacity to make amendments to bills and may defeat a bill that originated in the House of Commons such that the bill does not become law. While many Senate amendments to bills have been accepted by the House of Commons, the power of defeat has been sparingly used. Unlike in the United Kingdom, there is no legislation or formal agreement that restricts the function of the Senate. Instead, the Senate, by convention, invariably defers to the elected House of Commons, after bringing its concerns to the House of Commons and the public.

This result is consistent with the role of the Senate as the "complementary legislative body of sober second thought" and the Senate as the "conscience" of Parliament.

Legislating

While there are some bills that originate in the Senate, the majority of the time of the Senate allocated for legislation is spent considering government-sponsored bills that have passed through the three stages of legislating in the House of Commons. Once a bill has been passed by the House and is received by the clerk of the Senate, it will be introduced for first reading in the Senate by a senator. Like in the House of Commons, the first reading is *pro forma* and is adopted without debate. The second reading, committee study, and third reading follow a pattern similar to that of the House of Commons. Second reading involves a debate by senators on the principles and purposes of the bill. Following the vote on second reading, the bill is referred to the appropriate Senate committee, where witnesses are heard, amendments voted on, and the bill, as amended (if there are any amendments proposed and agreed to by the committee), is referred back to the Senate for third reading. If the bill is adopted at third reading in the same wording as passed in the House, the government requests the clerk of the Senate, acting in their role as clerk of the Parliaments, to make arrangements for royal assent.

The legislative work of the Senate as the complementary second legislative body provides a second look, or "sober second thought," that ensures better legislation. For example, the rights and interests that might have been lost or overlooked in the political expediency and partisanship of the House of Commons may be better protected by re-evaluation and amendment in the Senate.

Since most of the legislative work of the Senate is consideration of government-introduced legislation passed by the House of Commons, the focus of the Senate is quite different. Its primary function can be considered that of oversight, revision, and amendment. Generally, the Senate will not outright oppose legislation that has passed through the democratically elected and publicly accountable House of Commons. It does, however, consider whether the legislation was passed in haste or in a manner that failed to consider or account for the rights and interests of those who might be adversely affected by the legislation as passed in the House. The Senate then works to revise and improve the legislation to, among other things, address these concerns.

It is not uncommon for legislation to pass quickly through the House of Commons, possibly based on political considerations and through a whipped vote. The result can be a bill that was not fully vetted or considered by the House. But once the bill arrives in the Senate, it can be subject to more in-depth, less partisan consideration. Senate committees can call the witnesses that may have been denied an opportunity to appear before House committees, or who recognize "flaws" in the bill as passed in the House and want to bring their concerns to the Senate to support possible amendments. The makeup of the Senate also brings a different focus to the review of bills. Regional representation, personal expertise, and the voices of underrepresented groups ensures a potentially broader and differently focused review than that which a bill might have received in the House.

Since the government does not control the work of the Senate in the same way that it controls the agenda of the House of Commons, the Senate can take as much time as it considers appropriate to study bills. During this time, it can hold public meetings that expose the imperfections in bills. The delay, combined with the evidence heard by committees, often results in press coverage and public pressure being brought on the government to accept amendments proposed by the Senate. The tactic of delay to allow public pressure is one of the most effective tools that the Senate has to push for amendment of legislation.

The effectiveness of the entire process has been enhanced since the 2014 reforms to Senate appointments. As most senators are now independent of traditional party whips, there has been an increased number of amendments to bills passed by the Senate. Governments can no longer count on block votes to defeat amendments within committee or the full Senate. The government has to consider and be better prepared to address Senate concerns, which are often backed by a greater degree of public support.

If the Senate passes amendments to a bill, the bill as amended is returned to the House of Commons for reconsideration. Keeping in mind any public support for the amendments and the risk of further delay, the House will consider and vote on the amendments. If all amendments are accepted, arrangements for royal assent are made. If any of the amendments are not accepted, the bill will continue to pass from House to Senate until a final version is agreed upon, or until the bill with the "final" amendments is defeated in the Senate. In the vast majority of circumstances, the Senate will accept the "final" version of the bill as passed by the House of Commons, based on the acceptance of the fact that the House of Commons is elected and that the government will be held accountable by the electorate, or the courts, for any effects of the legislation.

While the Senate may not have gotten its way, it will have done its job.

In circumstances of urgency or where a matter is particularly complex, the Senate may consider a pre-study or concurrent committee proceedings while a bill is moving through the House of Commons. The evidence and reports of the Senate committee, including any identified concerns or proposed amendments, would be a matter of public record that the House or its committees would have available to it as the bill proceeds through the House. At the same time, the Senate committee would have the work of the House committee available to it. In effect, a lesser form of legislative "Ping-Pong" might result in a fully considered and reviewed bill being passed by the House and referred to the Senate. This can expedite the legislative processes when necessary.

It is also possible for the two Houses to establish a joint committee that will study an issue or proposed legislation. Joint committees are composed of an equal number of members and senators. The joint committee hears evidence that can be referred to in either House and issues reports to both Houses. The assumption is that the result will be a unified position on proposed resolution or legislation that can then pass quickly through both Houses with little further study. Such joint committees are rare, but they have been used effectively to consider major changes, including constitutional proposals and amendments.

Committees

Senate committees carry out functions similar to those of the House of Commons. They consider legislation and inquire into various aspects of government activity and policy. While the function may be similar, the tone and approach to the matters before the committee may have a different focus. As a revising chamber, and one that is less politically partisan, the inquiries may be less acrimonious and more focused on the issues since there is less concentration on potential electoral consequences. This provides Senate committees with the ability to focus on legislation as passed by the Commons, and the potential consequences of enactment. Senators can invite different witnesses than the Commons to bring different perspectives and suggested amendments. The degree to which senators see their role as protecting regional interests and underrepresented and marginalized groups' rights from majoritarian overreach will inform Senate committee proceedings. Evidence and recommendations of committees can often temper the effects of legislation that is overtly political, and which could have unintended consequences, or violate the constitutional rights of vulnerable individuals. When such consequences are considered and addressed, it can lead to amendments that allow the policy of the legislation to be promoted in a manner that balances constitutional rights and might protect the legislation from constitutional attack in the courts.

The accountability role of Senate committees can be quite different from that of the House of Commons. In contrast to the "short-term" focus of the committee work in the House of Commons, Senate committees often conduct longer-term, policy-focused studies that offer evidence and proposed solutions to systemic problems. For example, the Senate has established special committees on aging, poverty, science policy, health, and mass media. These studies have sometimes spanned Parliaments, with the committee picking up the study once a new Parliament is summoned following a general election for Members of Parliament. Committees can function across Parliaments and focus on policy reform. These longitudinal studies are enabled by the nature of the Senate and the fact that senators have long-term appointments. Unlike committees in the Commons, the membership in Senate committees is stable. In the Commons, committee membership changes dramatically following elections, based on the electoral outcomes. Membership in Commons committees depends on who may have been re-elected, whether former Members of Parliament are given new responsibilities in the Commons or government, finding roles for new members, and the relative strength of each caucus in the Commons. With the exception of retiring senators, the makeup of the Senate on the summoning of a new Parliament is the same as at dissolution. Membership on committees remains stable and often unchanged. Senators can sit on committees for extended periods of time, thus developing expertise and committee memory. Studies are not interrupted by elections or changes in political exigencies. Given that senators are not subject to the same political pressures, and that studies take place over time, their work on the special committees is seen as more comprehensive, more politically neutral, and better considered. The recommendations of these more substantive studies have resulted in expanded public awareness and discourse as well as foundations for longer-term changes in the development of government policy.

Independence of the Senate

The Senate is an independent component of Parliament. It is distinct from the House of Commons. It has its own rules, procedures, and administration. The Senate and senators enjoy the same privileges as the House of Commons and its members. Its work is similarly protected from interference by the courts and the government.

The work of the Senate as a reviewing and revising chamber for legislation, and its ability to carry out longer-term studies, both relatively free from the political and partisan pressures that underlie the work of the Commons, is essential to better law-making and policy development at the federal level.

CHAPTER SIX

The Queen as Represented by the Governor General

The third component of Parliament is the Queen. In formal terms, Parliament is sometimes referred to as the Queen in Parliament. All Acts of Parliament are made jointly by the Queen, as represented by the Governor General, the Senate, and the House of Commons. If the position of Governor General is vacant, or the Governor General is not able to act, their functions are carried out by the Chief Justice of Canada, acting as administrator.

Although many of the functions of the Governor General are often seen as mere formalities or as anachronistic, they have a real impact on how Parliament functions and the relationship between Parliament, particularly the House of Commons, and the government. Although the consequences are serious and real, the decisions of the Governor General are generally taken in what seems to be a routine manner. However, from time to time, a decision might not be as obvious and will be taken carefully and after consultation and consideration. One example of such a decision was that of Governor General Michaëlle Jean in 2008 when she had to deal with a request by the prime minister that Parliament be prorogued. There had been a proposed vote of non-confidence and the Governor General had to take into account the possibility of calling on the leader of the Opposition to form a coalition government. After careful consideration the request for prorogation was granted.

In most of their functions, Governors General are not free to exercise independent decision making. They act only on the advice or requests of the prime minister or Cabinet, and no one else. In their functions that relate to Parliament, this is not the case. Some decisions are taken at the request of the prime minister, some with the advice of the two Houses of Parliament, and some as an exercise of reserve powers, that is, on their own consideration.

Formation of Government

Before a Parliament meets following an election, the Governor General must decide who they will call on to be prime minister to form a government. This decision is one that the Governor General makes on their own, based on who they believe will be able to obtain the confidence, that is, the backing, of the House of Commons. In most cases this is evident from the election results. If one party has won a majority of seats the decision is clear. The leader of that party will be asked to form a government. Where a party has won a large plurality of seats, the leader of that party will usually be asked whether they believe they can command the confidence of the House, and if so, they will be asked to form a government. When the number of seats won is close, the decision will be more difficult and based on who the Governor General believes has the best chance of garnering the support of other party caucuses in the House. In such cases, it is not uncommon for the Governor General to meet with the prime minister who last had confidence in the previous House of Commons, who may suggest that they be given the opportunity to test the confidence of the House. In this case, the Governor General, by convention, will grant the request on the understanding that if the government loses an early vote of confidence, the Governor General will not dissolve Parliament. Rather, they will call on the leader of the Opposition or other parties to determine whether they are prepared to try to obtain the confidence of the House and form a government. The Governor General is free to reject the request of the prime minister (particularly if their party does not have the most seats in the House of Commons) and call on another party leader to form a government, but with the same proviso regarding a loss of an early confidence vote.

Summoning Parliament and the Speech from the Throne

Once a prime minister is in place, they will advise the Governor General on the date to summon Parliament. The Governor General will then have the necessary proclamation issued and the various summonses will be sent to members and senators. At the first sitting of Parliament the Governor General will read the Speech from the Throne in the Senate, outlining what their government hopes to achieve in the session of Parliament. While the speech is delivered in the first person, with the government and its agenda set out in terms of "my government," the speech is in fact written by the prime minister and their advisers. A Throne Speech is read at the beginning of each session of a Parliament.

Prorogation and Dissolution

Each Parliament is separate from other Parliaments, with a new Parliament established following every general election. For example, the election held on 20 September 2021, was for membership in the House of Commons for the 44th Parliament. A Parliament usually consists of a few sessions of roughly one-year to eighteen-months duration each.

To end a session, the prime minister will request the Governor General to prorogue Parliament. Prorogation ends the session of Parliament, thus ending all business before both the Senate and the House of Commons. In normal circumstances, the request for prorogation is made when the prime minister believes that the work set out in the Throne Speech has been dealt with, or that circumstances are such that the agenda of Parliament needs to be reset to meet changed circumstances. Sometimes prorogations will be requested when the prime minister decides to resign their leadership during a Parliament and a new leader is chosen who will then be asked to become prime minister. The new prime minister will request a prorogation to put their Cabinet in place and to fashion a Throne Speech to set out their agenda.

Until relatively recently, requests for prorogation were routinely granted on request. However, sometimes prime ministers have attempted to use prorogation for political rather than parliamentary purposes. For example, in 2008, the prime minister requested a prorogation to avoid a confidence vote and the possibility that their government would be replaced by a coalition government led by the leader of the Opposition. The Governor General granted the request after long consideration, and allegedly on condition that the government present a budget soon after recall, with the vote on the budget to be considered a confidence vote. The government subsequently won the budget vote and continued to govern.

In 2019, in the United Kingdom, the prime minister sought and received a prorogation, as Parliament was considering what to do about an impending Brexit deadline. The prorogation would have severely limited the time Parliament had to consider the matter. In a rare case, the Supreme Court of the United Kingdom reviewed the matter and determined that the prorogation was improperly requested since it would preclude Parliament being able to properly carry out its constitutional functions. The Court followed an earlier ruling that had found that Parliament had a major role to play in how the United Kingdom was to exit the European Union. Because of the improper purpose behind the request, the prorogation was declared a nullity.

While there is a proper place for prorogation, recent events, such as those outlined above, suggest that where a prime minister attempts to use prorogation to interfere with parliamentary scrutiny and accountability, or to preclude Parliament from carrying out essential and constitutionally required business, there is a possibility that the request might not be granted.

Dissolution ends a Parliament. Dissolution is granted by the Governor General at the request of the prime minister. At the time dissolution is granted, the Governor General will request the chief electoral officer to issues writs of election for a specific date for the general election, in accordance with the *Canada Elections Act*. The request for the dissolution of Parliament, and the issuing of writs for an election, will almost always be granted. The Governor General will consider not granting a request when there has been a recent election and there was uncertainty as to whether the prime minister was going to be able to obtain the confidence of the House of Commons. If a request for dissolution is not granted the Governor General will either ask for the resignation of the prime minister, or dismiss them, in order to call on another member (usually the leader of the Opposition) to form a government. If that person either indicates that they do not believe they can obtain the confidence of the House, or if their government subsequently loses a vote of confidence, dissolution will follow. Otherwise, the new prime minister will carry on governing.

In 2007, the *Canada Elections Act* was amended to prescribe a fixed four-year term for Parliament.[1] The intent of the legislation was to discourage the calling of snap elections at the whim of the prime minister. As a result, there has been some controversy regarding requests to dissolve Parliament for dates short of those set out in fixed date elections legislation. It is noted that, while there are fixed dates for elections set out as four years from the previous general election, there is also a provision that indicates that nothing in the Act precludes the discretion of the Governor General to dissolve Parliament earlier. Convention indicates that the discretion is exercised on the advice of the prime minister, except in extraordinary circumstances. While some might argue that the Governor General ought to consider and apply the Act, or at least its premise, in the exercise of their discretion to grant dissolution, Governors General are properly reluctant to become involved in political decisions or those that might cause legal, political, or constitutional "crises." In a democracy, it is believed best to let the electorate decide whether the request for a dissolution and election was a good decision by the prime minister.

In the absence of a suspicion that the power to request a prorogation or dissolution is being misused, the Governor General will accede to the request of the prime minister. The decision on the wisdom of the request is for the electorate, not the Governor General, to decide.

Royal Assent

Royal assent is the final step in a bill being enacted as an Act of Parliament. The Governor General, as the third component of Parliament, gives royal assent to bills that have been passed in identical form by both the Senate and the House of Commons. Although constitutionally possible, a refusal to give royal assent has not happened since the early eighteenth century in the United Kingdom. In Canada there is no case where a bill has been refused royal assent.

Unlike executive powers that are exercised by the Governor General on the advice of the prime minister or the Cabinet, the granting of royal assent is a legislative act. Royal assent is carried out on the advice of the Senate and House of Commons. The formulation for enactment is found in the Preamble to every Act of Parliament, which provides "Now, therefore, Her Majesty, by and with the advice and consent of the Senate and House of Commons of Canada, enacts as follows."

Since granting royal assent is a legislative or parliamentary function, not an executive one, royal assent is not subject to judicial review or to interference by the courts.

Royal assent can take place two ways in Canada. Until 2002, royal assent had to be given in Parliament assembled, with the Governor General personally attending. In the presence of the Senate and members of the House of Commons, who will have been summoned to the Senate chamber for that purpose, the clerk of the Senate, in their capacity as clerk of the Parliaments, presents the bill and asks that assent be granted. The Governor General then signifies assent. Where royal assent takes place by the Governor General personally attending in the Senate, the bill becomes law at the instant royal assent is granted. Since 2002, this method of assent is only required to take place in limited circumstances, although it can still be used at any time. Otherwise, royal assent can be given by written declaration. This process involves various officials, including the clerk of the Parliaments and a representative of the Privy Council, attending on the Governor General asking for royal assent on behalf of the two Houses. After the Governor General signifies assent, the clerks sign a declaration to that effect. A letter is sent to each Speaker who then reads the letter to their respective House. The bill only becomes law once the letters are read in each House (or deemed to have been read if tabled when a House is adjourned).

Other Functions Connected to Parliament

There are a few other functions of the Governor General that are directly related to Parliament.

Senators are appointed to the Senate by the Governor General, on the advice of the prime minister.

Federally appointed judges, which include Supreme Court justices, Superior Court and Appeal Court justices, and justices of the Federal Courts, cannot be removed from office by the government. They can only be removed from office by a joint resolution of the Senate and House of Commons directing the Governor General to dismiss the judge. The same is the case for certain officers of Parliament, particularly the chief electoral officer. To date this process of impeachment has not had to be exercised. Those individuals who have been faced with such parliamentary sanction have resigned before such a process has fully played out.

Finally, where the appropriate resolutions for constitutional amendments have been adopted by the required number of legislative assemblies, the House of Commons, and the Senate, the Governor General will issue the proclamation of constitutional amendment.

CHAPTER SEVEN

Final Thoughts

As stated by Winston Churchill in November 1947,

> Many forms of Government have been tried, and will be tried in this world of sin and woe. No one pretends that democracy is perfect or all-wise. Indeed it has been said that democracy is the worst form of Government except for all those other forms that have been tried from time to time.

One might add that the Westminster system of government that Canada shares with the United Kingdom is antiquated, awkward, and in need of update and improvement. But it is still one of the best forms of democracy. Its longevity, evolution, and flexibility are evidence of this.

It is suggested that the Westminster system compares favourably to various republican forms of government. In such models, where the branches of government are separate and distinct, the result is often one that produces divided government, with one party controlling the executive and another controlling the legislature. Further, fixed terms for each government do not allow for either continuous accountability or the ability to reset by way of elections to resolve an impasse.

Is the Canadian system perfect? No. Are there ways it can be improved to better meet the needs of the twenty-first century? Undoubtedly.

The Westminster system has evolved for the better part of 900 years, but there have been some solid building blocks upon which it rests — continuing accountability for government action; a focused and stable government with a strong and committed Opposition; and legislation based on a political agenda but honed by a second level of scrutiny.

It is hoped that this short book has provided insight into the basic way the Canadian version of Parliament has developed and currently works. It is further hoped that, in a modest way, it will allow for informed discussion of day-to-day politics and the examination of issues with a more critical understanding, as well as allow for reform that respects and builds on the values and principles fought for and developed over centuries as Parliament responds to the needs of an ever-evolving liberal democracy.

Notes

CHAPTER ONE | History and Overview

1   30 & 31 Vict, c 3 (UK).
2   See The National Archives, "Charter of the Forest, 1225," online: www.nationalarchives.gov.uk/education/resources/magna-carta/charter-forest-1225-westminster/.
3   (3 Edw I).
4   1 William & Mary Sess 2 c 2.
5   *Reform Act 1832*, 2 & 3 Wm IV, c 45.
6   Part I of the *Constitution Act, 1982*, being Schedule B to the *Canada Act 1982* (UK), 1982, c 11.

CHAPTER TWO | The Functions and Purposes of Parliament

1   1 William & Mary, Sess 2, c 2.
2   30 & 31 Vict, c 3 (UK).
3   Schedule B to the *Canada Act 1982* (UK), 1982, c 11.
4   Part I of the *Constitution Act, 1982*, being Schedule B to the *Canada Act 1982* (UK), 1982, c 11.
5   *Mikisew Cree First Nation v Canada (Governor General)*, 2018 SCC 40 at para 160.
6   *Vaid v Canada (House of Commons)*, 2005 SCC 30 at para 29.2 [note the references and citations to Erskine May and earlier Canadian texts] and para 41.
7   *The Privilege of Parliament Act*, 4 Hen 8, c 8, often referred to as *Strode's Act*.
8   RSC 1985, c P-1.

CHAPTER THREE | **Political Parties**

1   RSC 1985, c P-1.

CHAPTER FOUR | **House of Commons**

1   Part I of the *Constitution Act, 1982*, being Schedule B to the *Canada Act 1982* (UK), 1982, c 11.
2   House of Commons, *Conflict of Interest Code for Members of the House of Commons*, online: www.ourcommons.ca/procedure/standing-orders/appa1-e.html.
3   RSC 1985, c C-46.
4   RSC 1985, c P-1.
5   *Standing Orders of the House of Commons*, SO 108(1)(a).
6   30 & 31 Vict, c 3.
7   Above note 1.
8   Schedule B to the *Canada Act 1982* (UK), 1982, c 11.

CHAPTER FIVE | **Senate**

1   RSC 1985, c P-1.

CHAPTER SIX | **The Queen as Represented by the Governor General**

1   Section 56.1 of the *Election Acts* was added by SC 2007, c 10.

References

BAGEHOT, W. *The English Constitution* (Oxford: Oxford University Press, 1867).

BOSC, MARC & ANDRÉ GAGNON. *House of Commons Procedure and Practice*, 3d ed (2017), online: www.ourcommons.ca/procedure/ procedure-and-practice-3/index-e.html.

BRYANT, C. *Parliament: The Biography volume 1* (London: Doubleday, 2014).

———. *Parliament: The Biography volume 2* (London: Doubleday, 2014).

CAMPBELL, E. *Parliamentary Privilege* (Sydney: The Federation Press, 2003).

CANADIAN STUDY OF PARLIAMENT GROUP. *The Crown and Parliament* (Montreal: Éditions Yvon Blais, 2015).

CRAIG, GM (ED). *Lord Durham's Report* (Ottawa: Carleton University Press, 1963).

CREWE, E. *Commons and Lords: A Short Anthropology of Parliament* (London: Haus Publishing, 2015).

———. *Lord of Parliament: Manners, Rituals and Politics* (Manchester: University of Manchester Press, 2015).

FRANKS, C. *The Parliament of Canada* (Toronto: University of Toronto Press, 1987).

GILBERT, SC. *Parliament: Its History, Constitution and Practice 1295-1919* (London: Thornton Butterworth, 1919).

GOLDSWORTHY, J. *The Sovereignty of Parliament* (Oxford: Oxford University Press, 1999).

———. *Parliamentary Sovereignty: Contemporary Debates* (Cambridge: Cambridge University Press, 2010).

GORDON, M. *Parliamentary Sovereignty and the UK Constitution* (Oxford: Hart Publishing, 2015).

HORNE, ALEXANDER (ED), ET AL. *Parliament and the Law* (Oxford: Hart Publishing, 2013).

HORNE, ALEXANDER, GAVIN DREWRY & DAWN OLIVER (EDS). *The Law and Parliament* (London: Butterworths, 1998).

JENNINGS, SI. *Parliament*, 2d ed (Cambridge: Cambridge University Press, 1961).

MACFARLANE, E. *Constitutional Pariah: Reference re Senate Reform and the Future of Parliament* (Vancouver: University of British Columbia Press, 2021).

MADDICOTT, J. *The Origins of the English Parliament* (Oxford: Oxford University Press, 2010).

MANGOT, JP JOSEPH. *Parliamentary Immunity in Canada* (Toronto: LexisNexis Canada, 2016).

MALCOLMSON, PATRICK N & RM MYERS. *The Canadian Regime* (Peterborough, ON: Broadview Press, 1996).

MARLAND, A. *Whipped: Party Discipline in Canada* (Vancouver: University of British Columbia Press, 2020).

MARSDEN, P. *The Officers of the Commons 1363-1978* (London: Her Majesty's Stationary Office, 1979).

MASTERMAN, JH. *The House of Commons: Its Place on the National History* (London: John Murry, 1908).

MORRIS, C. *Parliamentary Elections, Representation and the Law* (Oxford: Hart Publishing, 2012).

NORTON, P. *Governing Britain: Parliament, Ministers and Our Ambiguous Constitution* (Manchester: Manchester University Press, 2020).

SMITH, DE. *The Canadian Senate in Bicameral Perspective* (Toronto: University of Toronto Press, 2003).

———. *The People's House of Commons: Theories of Democracy in Contention* (Toronto: University of Toronto Press, 2007).

———. *The Constitution in a Hall of Mirrors: Canada at 150* (Toronto: University of Toronto Press, 2017).

SUEUR, AH. *Parliament: Legislation and Accountability* (Oxford: Hart Publishing, 2016).

THORNE, SIR PETER, REVISED BY MICHAEL CUMMINS. *Serjeant for the Commons* (London: House of Commons Library Document 14, 1994).

TWOMEY, A. *The Veiled Sceptre: Reserve Powers of Heads of State in Westminister Systems* (Cambridge: Cambridge University Press, 2018).

WAITE, PETER B. *The Confederation Debates in the Province of Canada, 1865* (Toronto: McClelland and Stewart, 1963).

WEBBER, GRÉGOIRE, ET AL. *Legislated Rights: Securing Human Rights Through Legislation* (Cambridge: Cambridge University Press, 2018).

Index

oversees matters of national concern,
11
Parliament as focal point in, 25, 93.
See also Parliament of Canada
prevails during dissolution pursuant to caretaker convention, 80
relationship with Opposition, 40.
See also Opposition
Government, responsible, 8–9, 37, 58
Government, Westminster system
attributes of, 8, 10, 74, 113–14
parliamentary democracy, as, 1, 38
role of Opposition in, 55
Governor General
acting on advice of Cabinet, prime
minister, 88, 106
appointment of Senators, 15, 94
call to form government after election, 17, 26, 58, 106
calls for prorogation, dissolution,
and, 106, 108–110
delivery of Speech from the Throne, 86
grants royal assent to bills, 13, 30,
98, 110–11
involvement in political decision/
crises, 109
proclaiming constitutional amendments, 44, 111
removal of federally appointed
judges, 111
representing Queen in Canada, 12,
25–26, 75, 105

Hansard, 50, 77
House of Commons
accountable to electorate, 26
administrative independence of, 52,
54, 61, 77
centre of constitutional power, 7, 13
collective of democratically elected
members, 13, 16, 65
component of Parliament, as, 2, 25
determines who will govern and for
how long, 38–39, 58, 79–80

focused on passing bills, budgets,
estimates, 14, 65, 70, 88
holding government, prime minister to account, 14–15, 26, 54,
65, 70, 80
mirroring UK House of Commons,
10
political pressure/expediency of,
27–28, 37–38, 97, 99
politically motivated members in,
15–17
resources of to be used for non-
political activities, 73–74
role and function of clerks, officers,
59–60, 69, 78–79
standing committees of, 14, 41, 83
Standing Orders of, 41, 55, 72, 75,
83–84, 86–87, 90–91
House of Commons (UK)
elections standardized for, 8
parliamentary privilege in, 45,
48, 78
House of Lords (UK), 95

Information Commissioner, 42, 85

Jean, Michaëlle, request for prorogation in 2008, 105
Judges. *See also* Courts
ineligible to hold Commons seat, 67
neutral on bills or contemplated
decisions, as, 49
removal of, 25, 111

Legislation, federal
applied nationally, 70
based on political and policy
agenda of government, 30, 114
constitutional validity of, 22
federal bills on spending, tax introduced in House, 14, 31, 65, 98
legislative process for, 33–36, 79, 87.
See also Bills
royal assent for, 13, 16

statutes applied to Parliament, government, 48–50, 53
subject to judicial interpretation after enactment, 47, 52, 67
Legislation, regulatory
delegated or subordinate legislation, as, 31, 56
majority of legislation passed, 55
requiring consultation of those affected, 32
Lobbying, 72–73

Magna Carta (1215), 3, 4
Members of Parliament (MPs)
accountable to constituency electors, 23, 27, 38, 69
cease to be members at dissolution of Parliament, 19
constitutional and political functions of, 38, 66
deriving authority from Constitution, 69
independent members in, 60, 76
legislative role of, 28–36
ombudsmen for constituents, as, 71, 73
qualifications for candidacy, 67
representatives of political parties, as, 13, 57, 63, 69, 72
resources used for parliamentary functions, 62, 71, 73–74
selection from for Cabinet positions, 79. *See also* Cabinet (Ministers)
Mikisew Cree First Nation v Canada (Governor General), 115n5 (ch 2)
Minister of Finance, 86
Minister of Justice, 36, 51
Monarchy (UK), 5–6, 8, 13, 19, 58

Officers, House of Commons, 57, 59–62, 78–79
Officers, Parliament, 42–43, 79, 85, 111
Official Languages Commissioner, 85

Opposition
assignment of ministerial critics, 40
caucus membership of, 58–59
important to functioning of government, 40
independence of, 53
input on issues from party members, to, 63
leads in accountability, motions of non-confidence, 41, 80. See also Accountability; Confidence, in the government
participation on committees, 44
political responses of, 38
public understanding of, 2
role in Question Period, 81–83. *See also* Question Period
Opposition, leader of
appointing critics to government, 40
call to form government, 106–9
kicking off Question Period, 81
leader of party caucus, as, 76
member of Board of Internal Economy, as, 62
recognition of in House, 60
seating in House of Commons, 74

Parliament (UK), 5–7
Parliament of Canada
ability to place limits on *Charter* rights and freedoms, 50, 88
accountable to electorate for its activities, 23–24
component parts of, 12
constitutional supremacy of, 28
contempt of, 50
dissolution of, 18, 37, 106–7, 109
fixed four-year terms of, 109
holding federal government to account, 24, 52
independence of, lack of interference with, 7, 20, 23, 45, 52–53
language, culture, legal system context of, 1

About the Author

Steven Chaplin is a Fellow at the uOttawa Public Law Centre, and teaches Public Law, Constitutional Law, and the Law of Parliament at the Faculty of Law (Common Law), University of Ottawa. Formerly Senior Legal Counsel at the House of Commons, he is a Deputy Executive Editor of the Journal of Parliamentary and Political Law and has published numerous articles, book reviews, and book chapters, and maintains a blog at lexparl.com on the Law of Parliament.

About the Editor

Gregory Tardi, BCL, LLB, DJur, is the general editor of the Understanding Canada Collection. He is a member of the Barreau du Québec and serves both as president of the Institute of Parliamentary and Political Law and as editor of the *Journal of Parliamentary and Political Law*. He has served as legal counsel with Elections Canada and at the House of Commons. He has taught at McGill, York and Queen's universities and is the author of several books, including *The Theory and Practice of Political Law* and *Anatomy of an Election*.